Making
MUSICAL
Meaning

UNLOCKING THE VALUE OF MUSIC EDUCATION
IN THE AGE OF INNOVATION

Making
MUSICAL
Meaning

UNLOCKING THE VALUE OF MUSIC EDUCATION
IN THE AGE OF INNOVATION

ELIZABETH SOKOLOWSKI

GIA Publications
Chicago

Making Musical Meaning
Elizabeth Sokolowski

GIA Publications, Inc.
7404 S. Mason Ave.
Chicago, IL 60638
www.giamusic.com

G-8357

ISBN: 978-1-57999-915-5

Cover Design and Layout by Martha Chlipala

CHOICE

The art of teaching is about the art of giving...
Giving to others through your gifts and passions...
Giving to others with purpose, compassion, honesty
and humility.

Making Musical Meaning is the art of making *Music*...
Through the art of giving.

We teach Music because of *how* it makes us feel...
And *why* it makes us feel...

Teaching is a journey through time...
And as artist-musicians we intimately touch the souls of others...
For a lifetime.

You are the conduit to the world for your students...
Hold their hands and treasure their hearts...
And lead them on a remarkable and beautiful
journey through Music.

—CONTENTS—

— PART ONE—

EFFECTIVE ORGANIZATIONAL IMPACTS:

— PART TWO —

—FOREWORD—

BY DR. TIM LAUTZENHEISER

Elizabeth ("Beth") Sokolowski is a remarkable individual who stands at the forefront of the music education field. From teaching beginning instrumentalists to working alongside university music students prior to their entry into the profession (and everything in between), Beth has "done it all," and she has defined her own career with a trademark of signature excellence. She "walks her talk" with a sense of purpose-and-mission unknown in common hours; and—above all—Beth is an exemplary role model as a music learner, a music teacher, a music maker, and a MASTER EDUCATOR.

In the pages-to-follow you will quickly ascertain her passionate mission of quality music education for every child. This book is a reflection of Beth's own immeasurable drive to explain the elusive, wonderful magic of music. Moreover, she continues to challenge the reader to "make a choice" and completely commit—and connect—to the intrinsic joy of musical expression.

This is not a book you will read and then put on your library shelf, rather it is one you will read, re-read, study, think about, read again, and realize the knowledge shared is becoming a part of your artistic fabric. Embracing the relevance is only the gateway to the positive impact it will have on every aspect of your being, both professionally and personally.

Professor Sokolowski reminds all of us about the possibilities we all have within our grasp. Music isn't something we do, music is something we are, and nobody models this concept with more conviction than the book's author. You are about to go on a journey of unlimited potential; the message on-the-lines and the message between-the-lines is a rich treasure of immeasurable value. Enjoy it; be it...the choice is yours.

Dr. Tim Lautzenheiser is a clinician, author, and Vice President of Education for Conn-Selmer Inc.

—Acknowledgments—

It takes a whole village to raise a child...and I am so thankful for the support, love and guidance I have received through my journey.

First and foremost to my family...Dr. Robert Sokolowski, you are the finest and most dedicated educator, principal, scholar, husband and father. Your patience, understanding and support of my efforts and vision make this first attempt at writing a book possible. To my daughter Ana, you teach me new life lessons every day! My love for my child and being a Mom sets life into perspective and gives me purpose. I love both of you...*up to the moon and all the way back.*

To my parents, Marcel and Greta, who always saw the sky as the limit and allowed for me to reach for the stars and everything in life that I believed in.

To my sister, Jacqui...Love knows no time or distance. I miss you every day, but love you even more. Your strength and determination are an incredible inspiration to me.

To my friends and colleagues in the UArts community...Thank you for filling my life with beautiful music and artistry and for allowing me to contribute to such an incredible shaping of the future.

To my students...I learn so much from each of you, and I thank you for always pushing me to grow as a musician-educator. Your creativity, musicianship, and love for kids and teaching are refreshing and beautiful.

To Dr. Tim Lautzenhieser...I am so grateful for your support and care. As my guide and my light, you open doors for me to share what I believe in, what we believe in. Your insatiable passion and drive to impress upon the world that Music is essential in Education is a true inspiration.

To GIA Publications, NAfME, the Support Music Coalition (NAMM) and Conn-Selmer, Inc....Thank you for understanding and supporting the value of Music in Education.

To my friends and colleagues in the North Penn School District...Thank you for shaping my life, for showing me the way, for allowing me to be a part of an amazing music education faculty. Thank you for always believing in the potential of kids and the ways in which we can all make beautiful music together.

Finally, thank you to Edward S. Lisk. This book would not have come to fruition if not for you. As my mentor, teacher, and friend, you have filled me with confidence to share what I believe in. You nurture my teaching, cultivate my mind, and support my evolution as a musician-educator. You affirm for me the crystalline beauty of sharing MUSIC with our students. My words pale in comparison to what can be offered as a heartfelt thank you through music...if only this book could sing...I would improvise for you the most beautiful lullaby.

—INTRODUCTION—

Notes, like words, are mere utterances of symbols, and within themselves are totally lacking and incapable of expression. It is the human response, not [the] mechanical [one] that created the communication between the written symbol, the performer and the listener.

—William D. Revelli,
The Art of Cantando and Portamento in Wind Instrument Performance,
unpublished paper, from *On Becoming a Conductor* by Frank Battisti

Have you ever been to Florence, Italy and stood in front of David? Somehow he looks as if he breathes, as if his eyes connect with yours and his soul is touching yours. Michelangelo took an element completely solid and without feeling and he began to literally chip away at layers, to refine and shape, to create depth and texture of an earthly material that, for much of my life, I saw as a rock and nothing more. He was able to look beyond and see the potential, to understand the purpose and life and meaning in what for most of us remains a solid piece of marble.

I read an article describing the commissioning of David and how Michelangelo was not the original artist selected to complete the project. In fact the large piece of marble stood dormant, weathering the elements for many years, until he was awarded the commission to finish the project. This article detailed how David is typically depicted after the defeat of Goliath, but young Michelangelo offered a different depiction. The article added that his David is "a representation of the moment between conscious choice and conscious action." When I read this statement, the parallels of Michelangelo's perspective and how we approach music and education to me became significant, poignant, meaningful, and actually quite beautiful.

Experiencing David, on a hot summer day in Italy with forty 15-year-olds is one remarkable day in a larger puzzle of life, and as I think more deeply about the relationships and intangible connectivity of time, flow, energy and movement, this visual experience drew so many musical connections for me which have led to more questions than answers (a good thing!). This day and a handful of others inspire me to think about the profound means by which art—and most passionately for me music—communicates the soul of the human being and how I share these ideals with my students.

Through my journey, I have met many who have challenged me and opened up to me a musical world filled with passion and compassion, inspiration and understanding, meaning and purpose. I feel that I will never stop learning and growing, as the greatest gifts I have been given as a teacher are the opportunities to interact and grow with others in order to sculpt my life as musician, educator, and as a mother.

Making Musical Meaning is my philosophy of musical and educational convergence. It is the time and the place when I find purpose and am able to define for myself what music education is—at least for now. Music and education for me are constantly evolving. We sculpt them as we encounter life. As we grow as professionals, musicians, teachers, and as people so too does our means to bring music into the lives of our students. The ability as teachers to give to our students that which encompasses the beauty of music, the vision to design a music education program for the benefit of our students, and the realization that now more then ever we must understand our role and purpose as musician-educator, has brought me to attempt to put into words that which I feel can best be evidenced through music.

Music is the juxtaposition of the very personal residing within the universal. It is the culmination of our connections of heart, mind, body, spirit, and soul, originating in our "self" and emanating with and through others.

This approach to music education lives through two essential components: effective organizational impacts and affective lifelong potential. Effective organizational impacts are the means by which we as musician-educators design a comprehensive music education program for the benefit of our students. We have a necessity to deliver this musical learning while being cognizant of the affective lifelong potential that music can bring to our students. These two domains are creatively woven together, and are the foundation for my professional life as musician-educator.

In the onset of Daniel Pink's book, *A Whole New World*, he discusses the left and right hemispheres of the brain which are much like the context of the big idea for this book—there are two unique spheres of what we do, and yet they are inseparable. Pink quotes McManus:

> "However tempting it is to talk of right and left hemispheres in isolation, they are actually two half-brains, designed to work together as a smooth, single integrated whole in one entire complete brain. The left hemisphere knows how to handle logic and the right hemisphere knows about the world. Put the two together and one gets a powerful thinking machine. Use either on its own and the result can be bizarre or absurd." (p. 25)

This notion parallels the integration of effective organizational impacts and affective lifelong potential through music in education. Neither is mutually exclusive. One can not exist without the other. The symbiotic relationship of the effective and affective create meaning in music education.

WHY THE TERM MUSICIAN-EDUCATOR?

Throughout this book I will use the term *musician-educator* instead of *music educator*. The reason in simple. We were first musicians. We made a choice to teach. We could have chosen anything to teach, but we chose *music*, and in doing so we must never forget our musical identity. In our role as teacher, sometimes the musician can stand in the back as a distant representation of who we once were. I challenge you to never forget *why* you became a teacher...why you *chose* to become a musician-educator. We first loved music and had an insatiable passion for it. Then we chose to give this passion to others. Hold on to the *you* as musician, never let go of your musicianship and your love of what brought you to teaching.

WHY TEACH? AND WHY TEACH MUSIC?

If there is a person who stands at the front of that group of persons, then the humanity of that person is an important catalyst in the dynamic of musical creation.

Music in the classroom and ensembles can be "made" but it is created and generated from the very souls of those that produce it.

—James Jordan, *The Musician's Soul*

Teaching is a choice.
We choose *what* to teach.
We choose *how* to teach.
We choose *when* to teach.
We choose *where* to teach.
We choose...*why* we teach.

Take a moment and reflect upon the most memorable musical experience you have ever encountered. What was it that made it so memorable? Was there something about this experience that supported who you are today?

Why did you choose to teach? Why did you choose to teach music? Making meaning from our own experiences is one of the primary ways in which we can reflect and reflect often about the choices we make as musician and musician-educator. What influences brought us to where we are today and why do we do what we do? Our journey has sculpted who we are, and our musical, educational, and professional choices evolve our art of teaching.

Your most memorable musical experience may have been just that... an incredible performance opportunity. Your most memorable musical experience may have been the teacher and the inspiration who opened the door of music to your life.

In reflecting upon this experience, was there thought, contemplation, a process, or a design to the experience or the learning which authenticated it? Have you utilized or transferred this experience to your own life? To yourself, as musician? To your own teaching?

For me, the inspiration came from my middle school band director, Mr. Z. I loved playing the flute before entering the 6th grade, but my middle school years were the most formative and inspirational. A door to the world of music was opened through Mr. Z's teaching and love of music. In middle school, he created opportunities for us to be as musical as we wanted and to be engaged in playing music, and he dedicated himself to the art of teaching music. I knew by the end of middle school I wanted to be a music teacher. Mr. Z was my musical inspiration and my role model.

Mr. Z was the one who launched my musical career and modeled for me the qualities of an exceptional teacher. Through our journey of teaching the effective and affective domains of how we approach a musical education we are bound by the creativity that we possess and by the ways in which we actively seek ways to grow our programs for the benefit of our students. We must look beyond the roadblocks and bring solutions to the table for the sake of keeping music education a vital component of our student's lives, remembering that purpose-filled learning is a process and not an event. Not any one event can sustain our programs. It is our collective vision as musician-educators—and our deployment of this plan—that perpetuates music in our schools.

A new paradigm in teaching must be established as the shape of education changes. Our willingness to be active learners and to evolve from both the good and the bad is not only an example we need to set for our students, but a lifeline for the sustenance of our classrooms. As Randy Pausch says in his book, *The Last Lecture,* "Brick walls are there for a reason. They give us a chance to show how badly we want something." (p. 79) We must not let the negativity of what we hear and observe—and potentially disagree with—be our driving force. We must utilize that which we disagree with as a function to find and seek out that which we relate to, musically and educationally. This helps us to identify how we find meaning, value, and purpose in our classrooms and schools, and thus, how we affect change. When we find our vision, we find creative solutions to support students in their musical journeys.

Living in the negative experiences instead of *learning* and *growing* as a result of them overshadows the vibrant and musical educators we are. The life-giving and passion-filled classrooms that we create might be overshadowed by our feelings of helplessness. When we work conscientiously to continue our personal growth and to identify what we deem either valuable or lacking in our musical classrooms, we nurture our programs and the opportunities for our students to be engaged in meaningful and musically rich environments.

In the chapter *"Don't Complain, Just Work Harder,"* from Randy Pausch, he opens with this thought:

> "Too many people go through life complaining about their problems. I've always believed that if you took one-tenth the energy you put into complaining and applied it to solving the problem, you'd be surprised by how well things can work out." (p. 138)

We can easily identify a million roadblocks that stand in our way of meeting the musical needs of our students. What we do have control of are the creative choices we make to overcome these obstacles: the budget cuts, the program and course cuts, the lacking this and the no-more-existent that, and everything else that potentially stands in our way. Our future and the future of our students begins now. We choose *how* we will chart our future. Confucius said, "Our greatest glory is not in failing, but in rising every time we fall." How do we rise above adversity to ultimately make musical meaning? How do we utilize adversity as opportunity?

"We make a living by what we get, we make a lifetime by what we give." Churchill's statement is poignant and fitting as we reflect upon why we chose music. For most of us, the choice of music resides in the feelings created by giving music to others. For many of us, this is also why we chose the selfless act of teaching—to give to others what was once given to us.

In Ken Robinson's February 2010 TED Talk called *Bring on the Learning Revolution!* He says, "Life is not organic. We create our lives symbiotically as we explore our talents in relation to the circumstances they help to create for us." We chose music because somehow we connected with it in such a dramatic and passionate way that the choice was almost intrinsically made for us. What we did choose is to teach, and to teach music. In my office hangs a saying that I read every day as I open the door: "Do what you love and love what you do". At times the external factors take over our internal motivation and love for what we do. Discovering ways in which we can effectively manage the external so that our internal and day-to-day operations—teaching and music making— can be the meaningful influence that our students deserve is a priority.

My Story

I did it my way.

—written by Paul Anka
and sung by Frank Sinatra

A conductor's personal musical depth is critical to the success of the ensemble. As a conductor, your thinking, feeling, and musical expectations are all based upon your experiences.

—Edward S. Lisk,
The Musical Mind of the Creative Director

Here is my professional story...so far. I share this with you so that you may understand the whys and hows that brought me to identify and share a philosophical and reflective lens of music education. Like everything, these thoughts and perspectives will continue to evolve over time as the education system at the local, state, and federal levels change. As national education reform is impacted by diverse factors, and as my life as a musician and educator continues to blossom, so too does our theory emerge.

After graduating from Temple University in 1994, I accepted a position as a middle school band and general music teacher in the North Penn School District located in Lansdale, PA. This is a larger suburban school district, outside of Philadelphia, which serves 13,000 students in 17 diverse schools. My career began at Pennfield Middle School teaching 7th and 8th grade concert band and general music. In addition, I started a jazz lab band, as we had enough students beyond the jazz ensemble who wanted to learn and study music beyond the school day. I also taught marching band, several small woodwind ensembles, coached field hockey, basketball, and softball, and was the advisor for student council. After two years in the school district, and a major renovation of the old high school which became a middle school, I was transferred to Penndale Middle School. With renovations complete, three middle schools serving 7th, 8th and 9th grade students launched into action. I continued to teach 7th and 8th grade band and general music and to coach sports. Eventually I became department chair of the music program. I put myself on every committee I could volunteer for, and served on our effective schools' team and started an after-school tutoring club called START. After a colleague retired, I moved into the 9th grade band position and developed a pilot for a music technology lab, which was accepted and installed. At Penndale Middle School we developed a wind ensemble so that all students who had an interest in extending their skills beyond the curricular day could participate. This was in conjunction with the high school beginning a curricular wind ensemble. With the success we had at Penndale, music technology labs were installed at the other two middle schools and our general music curriculum moved into a hands-on environment, and wind ensembles developed at these schools as well. It was an exciting time in the school district! Our program was evolving.

I spent eleven years teaching middle school music and I loved every minute of it. Middle school, to me, is the hinge point. We nurture those who come to us from the elementary instrumental music program and we inspire our students to continue their study of music at the high school. Towards the end of my tenure at Penndale, I earned my Masters Degree in Educational Leadership from St. Joseph's University in Philadelphia and my supervisory and administrative certificate from the state of Pennsylvania. My husband had also completed this program and he was well on his way to becoming a principal. I was trying to figure out what was next for me. I think I am the epitome of "what's next."

Throughout my professional career, whether scheming up an idea for the classroom or the music program—or myself professionally—I seemed to have one foot in the present and an eye to the future. During my 11th year of teaching I spent time as an administrative assistant in the main office. While this was a very interesting position, I quickly figured out that music had to remain a component of my professional praxis.

At the end of that year a position at our school district's administrative office opened up for a coordinator of many of the special areas (K-12 Music, K-12 Art, Technology Education and Family and Consumer Science). I interviewed and got the position. It was the first time in my career I would be without students every day. This was a huge adjustment. This position as a learning coordinator was highly beneficial professionally. I was able to work for five years on "the other side" of education. When I left Penndale, my colleagues gave me a set of Star Wars figurines, as I was seemingly moving to the "dark side." These figures are with me to this day and remind me to always stay grounded in why I am an educator—to serve our students and to stay connected to them.

While working at district office, I had the honor of learning from some of the most talented educators and professionals. This wonderful group of learning coordinators were content experts in language arts, math, reading, library, special education, science, and social studies. Our original boss, the curriculum and data expert, brought an entirely new lens and scope on education into my life. These individuals opened my mind to the diverse world of education and modeled what it truly means to be a professional. They also brought a whole new perspective of public education into my life and a greater understanding of the complexity of American education. As my time in this position continued, I was given responsibility for supporting our secondary health teachers and the K-12 physical education program. With so many content area specialists to work with, I made the biggest realization of my educational career to date. These teachers who taught the other "specials" (I cannot stand this word) were passionate experts in their fields. I learned so much from them about their loves and interests and how they gave to students their lens of expertise. It made me realize that we all have gifts and talents to share with students, and the beauty of a holistic education is that students are immersed in many extraordinary experiences to help them identify where their creative potentials lie. I came to the realization that we are not specialists; we are essentialists. We bring to our schools and communities diverse environments where students can truly put their learning into creative and expressive practice.

Around the time that I took this position my husband had moved out of his teaching position as a Latin teacher and into the role of assistant principal and then principal. Clearly we are an "education family" and this has supported my growth and understanding of the educational spectrum. Both driven by our love and passion for learning, we regularly dialogue about the state of education. We share our fears, we discuss our vision and hope for the future, we celebrate the power that learning has in every child's life. On weekend evenings we dream our dreams about what education should be, and how we want to see education evolve and grow for the benefit of the students with whom we engage every day.

In 2009 a position for division head of music education opened at The University of the Arts in Philadelphia. I longed to be teaching again, and that "what's next" was that little voice in my head asking me where I was going. I updated my resume, had a lot of phone conversations with my mentors and colleagues who were teaching at the higher education level, and I decided I would apply. My interview was one of those magical days when I felt like my vision for music and education seemed to align beautifully with the committee I interviewed with. I thought to myself, "If I do not get this position, what I do know is that there are other musician-educators out there as passionate and energized by music as I am." A couple of weeks later, I accepted the position at The University of the Arts, accepting responsibility for the Music Education program. Higher education is yet another lens, and one very different from public education. My position is so fulfilling, and every day I am inspired by the future musician-educators with whom I share time in learning how to craft their skills as teachers of music.

I share my story because I think it is unique and also relevant. I have experienced music education from infant/preschool classes through the graduate level at this point in my life and there are as many similarities as differences! In living public education from such diverse lenses, I feel I have a strong grasp on what it takes to move music education forward. In the higher education role these days, my past experience in public education supports me in the training and teaching of future musician-educators, as I know what it will take for them to be successful out the door after graduation in securing a teaching position and living up to it's expectations and responsibilities.

These life, learning, and professional growth lessons have come through trial and error, and from inspiration and guidance from my mentors and teachers. I firmly believe that behind every ounce of success are countless hours of thought, contemplation, research, insight, organization, and strategizing so that the delivery of vision is exquisite. There are also incredible individuals who nurture our growth. No man or woman is an island. We truly need each other. Effective organizational impacts: a roadmap to create vision is where we can begin. There are rich tools and ways to answer the *how* and *why* questions of musical learning to make our vision reality.

Disclaimer: This next section of the book may be perceived as rather dry, so hang in there! Use this section of the book wisely to inform the change you want to make manifest in your professional praxis and school system.

—PART ONE—

EFFECTIVE ORGANIZATIONAL IMPACTS: A ROADMAP TO CREATE VISION

If I had 8 hours to chop down a tree, I'd spend 6 hours sharpening the axe.

—Abraham Lincoln

Effective Organizational Impacts addresses the components of a comprehensive music education program, how we as a department create our vision for musical learning, and why this is vital to the sustenance and growth of our classrooms. As a collective vision for a music education program is developed, equity through all facets of the program can be addressed. The landscape is changing, and we must be informed professionals in the larger context of education. The fiscal, social, technological, educational, and administrative realities have created a tenuous climate. How will we choose to lead? What will we do to ensure music is an essential component of the architecture of education?

An important understanding in creating a program vision, is to understand the tenets of current educational research, and how music plays a role in driving the influence of these initiatives throughout the system. It is critical that music education program leaders are informed, and make connections between today's educational imperatives and music.

There are a number of researchers, scholars, and models, which are vital to have an awareness of, and how they are threaded into who we are and what we do in music education.

The following notable educators, researchers and models have influenced and transformed an awareness of our role as musician-educators in our school communities. The ways in which we develop our teaching to best support student learning are musts in today's educational world.

Bloom's Taxonomy

In the 1950's, Benjamin Bloom, an educational psychologist, and a team of researchers determined that there are three psychological domains to learning: cognitive, affective, and psychomotor. "Originally developed as a method of classifying educational goals for student performance evaluation, Bloom's Taxonomy has been revised over the years and is still utilized in education today." (Heather Coffey, http://www.learnnc.org/lp/pages/4719) His team developed a taxonomy of learning based in the cognitive domain of knowledge. This hierarchy outlines a progression of higher order thinking skills. There are two models of the taxonomy (shown on the next page). The original was published in the 1950's and a second model was updated from the 1990's which a former student of Bloom's developed to reflect 21st Century learning skills. The updated taxonomy moves from using nouns as descriptors to verbs which identify active and engaged cognitive learning processes. Here are both original and revised versions side by side for comparison. The lowest orders of the taxonomy are in the last cells of the table moving up through the taxonomy through the top of the table.

Bloom's Taxonomy (1950's)	Updated Taxonomy (1990's)
Evaluation	Creating
Synthesis	Evaluating
Analysis	Analyzing
Application	Applying
Comprehension	Understanding
Knowledge	Remembering

Another model/adaptation more clearly supports language established by Grant Wiggins in the Understanding by Design curricular model, which is fundamental to quality lesson design. The idea is to identify the skills and knowledge being taught, and to be cognizant of how we as teachers can stretch the learning, moving beyond mere skills and knowledge and into comprehension and application. From here we identify how we will assess learning by stating the evidence of understanding.

Updated Taxonomy (1990's)
Creating
Evaluating
Analyzing
Applying
Understanding
Remembering

HERE'S AN EXAMPLE OF WORKING THROUGH THE TAXONOMY...

An objective for an instrumental music lesson is to learn and use the A-flat major scale. Perhaps this is due to the fact that one of the pieces of music being studied is in this tonality. The initial process is to learn the scale (knowledge and skills). To do so, the student will utilize the four-step process of scale mastery designed by Edward S. Lisk. This can be found in his series, *The Creative Director Alternative Rehearsal Techniques*. Once the scale is learned (knowing) and the student can play the scale without error (comprehending) the student can now apply the scale to a piece of music being played in this key (applying). Through analyzing the piece of music, the key signature, significant elements of the melodic contour of the music, and ascending and descending technical passages throughout the piece of music, the student identifies the larger understandings of the piece of music (analyzing and synthesizing). As the student plays the piece of music and records his/her rehearsal, active listening can be engaged to evaluate the performance of the music, and a self-reflective assessment of the strengths and needs can be made (evaluating). Finally, as an extension, and to move to the highest cognitive level of the hierarchy, the student can then create a beautiful melody in the key of A-flat major, played freely on their instrument, with inflection, nuance and meaning.

Here is a visual of the process. Note that the visual begins with the lowest point of the taxonomy at the bottom of the table and moves up in sophistication and maturation.

Adaptation of Bloom's Taxonomy	Example
Creating	Creating a beautiful melody on one's instrument using the scale/tonality
Evaluating	Recording and then self-assessing through active listening the utilization of the scale/ tonality appropriately throughout the performance of the repertoire
Analyzing and Synthesizing	Observing the melodic and technical aspects of the repertoire in relation to the scale/tonality
Applying	Reading/Connecting the notation for the sale to playing the scale effectively
Comprehending	Playing the scale correctly
Knowing	Learning to play a scale utilizing the musical alphabet

When we design learning which is transparent, connects to standards and intellectual/cognitive growth and development, and identifies clearly the rigorous and relevant process of making meaning through music, we substantiate a comprehensive learning process which engages both left and right brain activity. What is critical to such teaching is the design process. If we extend this one simple example of learning a scale to how we envision and deploy the larger context of learning in our coursework, how we deliver this quality instruction to our students, and to the means by which we create a rigorous and relevant learning environment, we are then teaching through the four domains of professional practice established by Charlotte Danielson.

A PROFESSIONAL FRAMEWORK FOR TEACHING

Charlotte Danielson's study of teaching and learning has led to the development of her framework for teaching, which is rooted in four domains of professional practice.

- Domain 1: Planning and Preparation
- Domain 2: The Classroom Environment
- Domain 3: Instruction
- Domain 4: Professionalism

Danielson states,

> The framework for teaching...identifies those aspects of a teacher's responsibilities that have been documented through empirical studies and theoretical research as promoting improved student learning. Although they are not the only possible description of practice, these responsibilities seek to define what teachers should know and be able to do in the exercise of their profession. (page 1)

These four domains are threaded through all we do as educators, whether made transparently evident or not. Currently the four domains of professional practice are the evaluation domains for the state teacher and student teacher formal evaluations in Pennsylvania. Knowing and understanding the domains, our ability to design our programs in support of these domains, and the ways we make evident that rigorous and relevant teaching is occurring in our musical classrooms in support of student learning, substantiate what we do and why music is essential in education. The domains are the foundation from which our study and deployment of teaching begins. A great way to utilize the four domains of professional practice in our music education programs is to write our annual teaching goals and professional portfolio through the framework. Creating awareness of the domains and then sharing our goals with systems administrators—making evident our knowledge and use of the four domains of professional practice—evidences the music education program's collaborative efforts toward teaching through research based educational criteria.

Planning and Preparation is both the starting and ending point for a lesson. Teaching needs to begin somewhere in order to develop and refine learning over time. As a teacher we need to not only have the knowledge but we must be able to apply and demonstrate this learning in an active and engaging classroom. Planning and preparation begin with a design of something concrete and deals with the *what* of what is being taught, and more importantly the *how* of the teaching and learning.

Classroom Environment involves creating an environment of respect and rapport, establishing a culture for learning, having clear classroom procedures, being cognizant of student behavior and management, and involves the organization of physical space to support learning. Students remember their teachers by how they the students are treated and the environments in which learning is both energizing and safe. Students engage in classrooms where they are seen and treated as real people with interests, concerns, and intellectual potential. Classroom environment involves the physical structure and space as well as the thinking/feeling/meaning/value-oriented components of our classrooms.

Instructional Delivery means, "can you play the gig!" Our delivery is critical to students not only "doing" the material but beyond this... *learning* and *understanding* the material. There is a big difference between active participation—or the doing—and authentic knowing. Instructional delivery is the fulfillment of what we plan and prepare for in domain 1. Domain 1 is prep for domain 3. Instructional delivery focuses on the effective communication with students: the use of quality questioning and "deep" discussion techniques which engage students in learning. This domain also includes the use of assessment in instruction for the purpose of learning. When teachers demonstrate flexibility and responsiveness to support student learning we adapt to the needs of learning to benefit students.

Professionalism...It's all about *us!* Our communication with the community and parents is a factor that distinguishes us from less proficient teachers and colleagues. Domain 4 allows for reflection on teaching, and acting on these reflections to make our teaching and our classrooms better. It is the ability to maintain accurate records and to communicate with families. The participation in a professional community and how we grow and develop, as educators, are inclusive of this domain. Finally, how we show our professionalism is critical, and this means in ALL facets of our representation of our school. From grooming, dressing, how we relate and react to others (teachers, students, administrators, parents), our communication skills with all stakeholders (anyone you impact through your teaching), and our rapport with others all impact how we are defined as teaching professionals.

On Rigor and Relevance

Rigor and Relevance are two words primary to education in the 21st Century. Having a working knowledge of the research and tools of Willard Daggett and Robert Marzano are essential in today's educational spectrum. "The Rigor and Relevance Framework is a tool developed by the staff of the International Center for Leadership in Education to examine curriculum, instruction, and assessment. The Rigor and Relevance Framework is based on two dimensions of higher standards and student achievement." These two standards, which are Bloom's Taxonomy and deemed the application model, are examined on an x-y coordinate graph to chart four quadrants of learning. Rooted in the research of Willard Daggett, notable educational scholar, more information about the framework can be found at www.leadered.com. This model will be explained in relation to musical learning in greater depth in the section entitled Cultivating Ownership.

DEFINING AND APPLYING HIGH-YIELD STRATEGIES

Robert Marzano, Debra Pickering, and Jane Pollack, in the book *Classroom Instruction that Works*, identify high yield and research-based strategies to increase student achievement. There are a myriad of ways in which these strategies connect to the music education classroom. As we reflect upon the strategies, we should make connections to our teaching and learning environments.

1. **Identifying similarities and differences** - Performing mental operations which are a component of basic human thought. These can include being able to compare, classify, and decipher and employ metaphor and analogy.

    Example: In this example, students are asked to be active listeners in a general music classroom. Students are provided with a three-column paper (one for each listening excerpt). They are asked to write down their observations of the excerpts as they listen. Three excerpts of pieces of music are played for the class. In the front of the classroom are three large pieces of paper. Students are asked to write their observations on the pieces of paper, and to also review what their peers have written. If one of their ideas has been similarly stated by another classmate, they are to place a star by that statement.

Once students have completed reporting out, the class discusses their observations. Then the teacher either begins two new pieces of paper or utilizes another writing space with two columns. From the initial observing and recording to the reporting out and the class discussion, the whole class is now engaged in identifying similarities and differences in the three excerpts.

In this example, the class has then done the following:

- Engaged in active listening
- Organized their observations through writing
- Discussed their feedback
- Identified similarities and differences

In regard to Bloom's Taxonomy, this has brought students out of skills and knowledge, and into comprehending, applying, synthesizing, and evaluating—all higher order thinking skills.

2. **Summarizing and note-taking** - "To effectively summarize, students must delete some information, substitute some information, and keep some information." (*Classroom Instruction that Works,* Marzano, Pickering, and Pollock, p. 30) The idea is for students to understand the qualitative nature of summarizing and to use their note- taking skills as a study aid.

Example: In a music technology class, students are making a podcast about a composer or performer that they admire. Their podcast is to include biographical information about the composer, as well as audio and visuals to support the life and times of the individual they have chosen. In their research phase, the ability to summarize information gathered and to report out on the essential facts and significant events in this individual's career are the goals. The ability to synthesize their research findings and creatively summarize not only in words, but through visual and audio supplements, takes this one dimensional high yield strategy into a three-dimensional learning environment.

3. **Reinforcing Effort and Providing Recognition** - We support student learning when we model, teach, and acknowledge the effort that is utilized to arrive at a quality outcome. Positive feedback given is often most effective when displayed as meaningful achievement.

    Example: Formative assessment is an essential component of the ensemble classroom. Assessment begins with identifying a problem or concern, but the specific and timely feedback which activates a change in the learning is the critical stage. Instead of shouting out random bits of feedback while students are engaged in playing, instead give feedback when the students can actively listen to what you have to say; meaning not *while* they are playing, but *after.* If students are to effectively incorporate your feedback, then they must be given the opportunity to listen to and respond to your feedback. When we reinforce effort by first assessing and providing feedback, and then by acknowledging a quality performance, we alert our students to tangible ensemble goals and expectations.

4. **Homework and Practice** - Focused practice is essential to strengthen understanding and to secure and master knowledge and skills. Research suggests that homework is most effective when there is purpose, when it is independent, and when teacher feedback is provided.

    Example: Give students specifics about what to practice and review your expectations. Strategy #4 strongly relates to #3. Students must know what to practice, but more importantly how to practice. They must understand the goal of this focused practice in order to grow as a musician and meet expectations. This goal leads to efficiency in learning. When students know and understand what to practice, chances are they will return to the ensemble prepared. The teacher has also built in the expectation that students will come to the following rehearsal prepared, having focused on purposeful practice.

5. **Nonlinguistic Representation** - Students are able to represent knowledge in a form other than words; for example, using graphic organizers, mental pictures, and through kinesthetic activity.

   Example: Engaging in making music. When students are actively immersed in making music, formally or informally, with or without notation, through singing, movement or playing instruments, they are learning through non-linguistic representation.

6. **Cooperative Learning** - Students work interactively to promote positive independence, interaction, accountability, and developing intrapersonal and group processing skills. The deployment of cooperative learning must be planned, consistent, and systematic.

   Example: Ensemble opportunities for all students...collective, collaborative, and cooperative experiences! A music education program is most effective when it reaches all learners in a school. Beyond the traditional ensembles which certain students show interest in (band, chorus, orchestra), find new ways in general music class or through alternative ensembles to engage students who might not normally perceive themselves as musical or even having an interest in music. When we collaborate and cooperate through music, life-long social and communicative skills are developed as well as foundational musical skills, and an appreciation for the arts.

7. **Setting Objectives and Providing Feedback** - Objectives establish the *why* of learning and provide focus. Specific, corrective, and timely feedback through formative assessment strategies are vital to student growth.
   Example: Set goals and objectives for each lesson or rehearsal that we engage in, and make these goals evident and transparent to students.

Learning should not be a mystery! Tell students what they should know and what they should be able to do.

8. **Generating and Testing Hypotheses** - This is the application of knowledge in two ways. The first is to induce or draw new conclusions from given information and the second is to deduce by using a rule or by making a prediction about a future event or action. To authenticate the act of hypothesizing, teachers must ask for clarification. The understanding is in the justification of the measure.

   Example: When working with his students and a question was asked, Stephen Melillo would often respond to his students "Let's Find Out!" If we want to engage our students in an active and creative musical process, they must feel as though they are stakeholders in the learning. Our role as teacher is to move beyond the telling and into the teaching, so involve your students in the process and support them in their discovery of musical understanding by helping them to uncover the beauty of music!

9. **Cues, Questions and Advance Organizers** - Cues and questions help students to retrieve what they already know by activating prior knowledge. Quality questioning provides focus. Higher level questions (think Bloom's) results in a deeper level of learning. Advance organizers are a means to organize thinking and recall which leads to deeper understanding.

   Example: In an ensemble setting, we create value and ownership of the music making by engaging students as active participants. We must support them as consistent active listeners in the ensemble as well. Asking quality questions to activate observation skills as well as the recall of prior knowledge is paramount to musical growth. Prompting questions and recall skills activate prior experiences and dig deeper to allow for students to become more mature and sophisticated makers of music. This establishes a high level of rigor and relevance in our classroom. Advance organizers are an effective tool for students to understand the plan for a concert. Have you ever given an ensemble the order of the concert, and then asked them to map, in their own words, why the repertoire is in this order? To dig deeper and make connections between thoughtful planning for a concert and the established goals for your ensemble, have students engage in this type of exercise and discuss their feedback. See if they understand the connections between the literature selected, and the order in which the concert is being played. This type of conceptualization takes learners to the higher levels of Bloom's. Students are synthesizing and analyzing the connectivity of the larger plan, and making meaning of their learning. Create learning for a purpose and make it evident!

When we successfully identify and evidence the inclusion of the high yield strategies in our planning, preparation, teaching, and student work, we are clarifying that the music education program understands the value of current educational research and the means to support authentic student learning. A great inservice exercise is to create awareness and understanding of the high yield strategies, to be able to define the strategies in our own words, and to make evident the meaningful ways in which we use these strategies in teaching and learning music. Share your outcomes with systems administrators in a well prepared document to substantiate how these strategies support music in education.

UNDERSTANDING BY DESIGN

The Understanding by Design (UbD) model created by Grant Wiggins and Jay McTighe is one of the most significant components of today's educational fabric. It has made a serious impact upon the ways in which the design of teaching and learning has been transformed. UbD is based in student inquiry and the design of curriculum, instruction and assessment. The transfer of learning—or being able to take what you have learned and apply it to other places, situations, or contexts—is fundamental to this process. Student learning matures through acquiring knowledge, making meaning of learning, and transferring this learning to broader and more sophisticated contexts. The outcome? We create learning for purpose. In the program development portion of this book you will gain an understanding of how UbD can be utilized to effectively design a cohesive music education program.

The ability to teach in a way that frees students to use their knowledge in meaningful ways, is the heart of this process, and thus the heart of thoughtful design of our lesson plans, our curriculum, and our program. Bransford, Brown and Cocking in How People Learn state, "students develop flexible understanding of when, where, why and how to use their knowledge to solve problems if they learn how to extract underlying principles and themes from their learning experiences." (2000, p. 224) The question is then, at all levels and in all facets of our music education programs, do we approach the design of our music education programs in this way?

ESSENTIAL TERMINOLOGY FOR PROGRAM DESIGN

Design - "to have purposes and intentions; to plan and execute" (Oxford English Dictionary)

Standards - "Standards provide a framework for us to identify teaching and learning priorities and to guide our design of curriculum and assessments." (UbD, p. 14).

Understanding - "is to make connections and bind together our knowledge into something that makes sense of things." "To be able to understand is to be able to wisely and effectively use—transfer—what we know, in context; to apply knowledge and skills effectively, in realistic tasks and settings." "To understand means that we show evidence of being able to transfer what we know." (UbD, p. 7)

Transfer - "involves figuring out which knowledge and skills matters here and adapting what we know to address the learning at hand." (UbD, pg. 41)

Evidence - "we need to see evidence of students' ability to 'extract' understandings and apply them in situated problems, in performance—something quite different from merely seeing if they can recall and 'plug in' the underlying principles." (UbD, pg. 49)

Big Ideas - establish learning priorities. Big ideas bring together related content knowledge, provide focus and a lasting value to the learning, are at the core of a subject, need to be uncovered, are hard won results of inquiry, are not obvious, and are abstract and conceptual in nature. Wiggins states that big ideas "provide a focusing conceptual 'lens'... point to ideas at the heart of expert understanding of a subject...and have great transfer value." (UbD pg. 69)

Enduring Understandings - identify what students will know, understand and be able to do in the context of the big idea.

Knowledge and Skills - target the specific skills/knowledge/content which will be mastered/secured in order to reach our overarching goals. "Knowledge and skills are necessary elements of understanding, but not sufficient in themselves." (UbD, pg. 41)

DIFFERENCE BETWEEN KNOWLEDGE AND UNDERSTANDING

Knowledge	Understanding
The facts	The meaning of the facts
A body of coherent facts	The "theory" that provides coherence and meaning to those discrete facts
Right or wrong	A matter of degree or sophistication
I know something to be true	I understand why it is... what makes it knowledge?
Concrete	Conceptual

The final component of the teaching-learning process to make evident is connectivity between Bloom's Taxonony and UbD. Bloom states, "Understanding is the ability to marshall skills and facts wisely and appropriately through effective application, analysis, synthesis, and evaluation." (Bloom, 1956). When we thread the ideals of the taxonomy with those of the Understanding by Design model, a congruent teaching-learning model is fully realized in which the maturation and sophistication of the learning hierarchy is synthesized with an effective teaching process. This visual provides a convergence of the taxonomy and the UbD process. You will observe in the graphic that Bloom's Taxonomy is inverted. The purpose for this is that much of learning gets "stuck" in the lower levels of cognitive function in the taxonomy, living in mere knowledge and skills, void of meaning and purpose. The inverted visual provides a flow and energy, aligned with UbD, to move us out of mere skills and knowledge and into active engagement of mature and complex cognition for all learners of all ages. While never explicitly stated, the intention of having students learn through Bloom's hierarchy of learning is to create purpose.

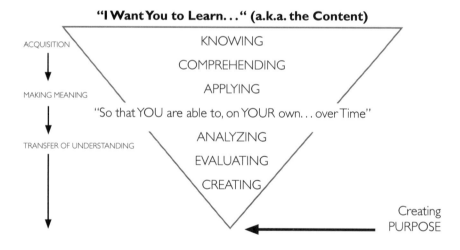

An excellent example of the employment of the Understanding by Design model to clarify standards based education is the New Jersey Standards Clarification Project. The Visual and Performing Arts document can be viewed here: http://www.state.nj.us/education/aps/njscp/Phase1allAreas.pdf#page=1. This project identifies a mission statement for each content area (or groups of content areas, as in the visual and performing arts model) and then uses the specific state standards to align a big idea, essential questions, and enduring understandings. The thoughtful design of this project for the visual and performing arts provides clarity and a vision for the effective implementation of a standards-based model for curricular planning.

QUALITY LESSON DESIGN

You are the Creative Director and it is your responsibility to shape and design a rehearsal that helps your ensemble achieve the results you anticipate.

—*Edward S. Lisk,* The Musical Mind of
the Creative Director

Quality lesson design is imperative to quality teaching. Lesson design involves the MACRO of year-long or years-long planning, to the MICRO of day-to-day planning. Lesson design is fundamental to planning and preparation, one of the four domains of professional practice. Planning and preparation is a non-negotiable. It begins with our Big Idea, our broad conceptualization of how learning will be focused and organized for our students in a given school year. In an ensemble classroom, this is rooted in the repertoire we program. As we carefully select literature for the concerts our ensembles will present, we begin to identify the enduring understandings which connect the literature to the curriculum we are responsible for teaching. This large-scale planning connects the discrete skills and knowledge which are benchmarked for study and mastery in the curriculum for that ensemble. This also provides a transparency to the learning which students can readily identify throughout the academic year. Once literature is carefully planned for the year and concerts are finalized, the work to design and plan for daily lessons can begin. Strong pedagogical foundations that support the repertoire are essential to learning. A consistent lesson design process is important. This does not mean that every ensemble rehearsal is the same; it means that fundamental domains of planning are fulfilled for each lesson to support the learning goals. Lesson design that is standards-based evidences the curricular relevance of what we are teaching and why.

Goals and objectives give purpose and focus to a lesson and answer the question, "What should students know, understand and be able to do at the conclusion of the lesson?"

Evidence of understanding is the assessment measure, whether formative or summative, which indicates whether the goals and objectives have been met. Identifying evidence can be accomplished by answering the questions, "How will you know that students understand the objective(s)?" and/or "What is the evidence of understanding?"

Introduction/warm-up to the lesson identifies the strategies that will be used to begin the lesson. It is essential to connect what occurs at the beginning of the class/rehearsal to the body of what will be learned and understood. Questions such as, "What strategies will you use to begin the lesson, and why?" and "How is the warm-up tied to the body of the lesson?" can be used to prompt planning.

Body of the lesson is content and objective specific. It details how the content skills and concepts to be learned and understood will be taught, not simply what will be taught. Student engagement is critical. A carefully detailed lesson is respectful to an efficient learning process. As time is a priceless commodity for many of us, careful planning and preparation will help us to use our rehearsal time to the fullest.

Conclusion/wrap-up is the culminating portion of the lesson when we can formatively assess whether or not students have met the objectives of the design. This is where evidence is lived and understanding is displayed as knowing beyond mere doing. Prompting questions to support the plan for the end of the class are "How will we conclude the lesson?", "How will students make evident that they understand the objective(s) of the lesson?", "How will we know?", "How will students show that they know?", "How will we check for understanding?"

Lesson design in 21st Century education is standards-based. Knowing and understanding the National Standards for Music Education and the state standards for Music Education are essential. In some states, standards for music education are a component of a larger Arts and Humanities initiative. Draw connections between national and state standards, and make this crosswalk evident in your planning. The National Standards for Music Education often provide the clarity and specificity in support of the state standards. Some states have written a crosswalks document to bridge the national arts standards with state standards. As the Understanding by Design model has been embraced by states, standards models have transitioned into multi-faceted standards aligned systems, which emanate from the goal of student achievement. The Pennsylvania Standards Aligned System is one such model. It is focused on student achievement supported by clear standards, fair assessments, curriculum framework, instruction, materials and resources, and interventions. State Department of Education standards models are becoming much more sophisticated and in depth. It is important to maintain awareness of the maturation of these standards-based frameworks, and to draw connections to our curricular framework.

University of the Arts Sample Ensemble Lesson Plan Template

UArts School of Music Lesson Plan Design Template	
Focus: concepts and skills to emphasize Rhythmic Melodic Singing Listening Form and Function Harmony Moving/Kinesthetic Creating Tone Color Improvising Expressive Qualities Vocabulary Playing Instruments Composing Music History Music Theory Evaluating and Analyzing Music Musical Symbols (Reading and Notating)	**Grade Level:** _____ **Course:** _____ == **Objectives** (give PURPOSE and FOCUS to a lesson): What should the students know, understand and be able to do at the conclusion of this lesson?
Materials/Equipment:	**Evidence of Understanding:** How will you know that students understand the objective(s)? What is your *evidence* of understanding?
National Music Standards Achieved: - Singing, alone and with others, a varied repertoire of music - Performing on instruments, along and with others, a varied repertoire of music - Improvising melodies, variations and accompaniments - Composing and arranging music within specific guidelines - Reading and notating music - Listening to, analyzing, and describing music - Evaluating music and music performances - Understanding relationships between music, the other arts and disciplines outside the arts - Understanding music in relation to history and culture	**Lesson Design:** **Introduction of Learning:** What strategies will you use to begin the lesson? And why? How is the introduction tied to the body of the lesson?
Bloom's Taxonomy Creating Evaluating Analyzing and Synthesizing Applying Comprehending Knowing	**Body of the Lesson:** Outline the "body" of the lesson... make sure it is content and objective specific... make sure you detail HOW you will teach the content, skills, concepts you want the students to know and understand... not just WHAT you will teach.
Differentiated Learning: Auditory Visual/Spatial Kinesthetic Logical/Mathematical Musical Verbal/Linguistic Naturalistic Interpersonal Intrapersonal	
Classroom Strategies: Technology Writing/Reading Charts/Graphs/Maps Hands-On/Problem Solving	
DATE:	**Conclusion/Wrap-up:** How will you conclude the lesson? How will the students make evident that they understand the objective(s) of the lesson? How will you check for understanding?

Designed by The University of the Arts Music Education Division (Elizabeth Sokolowski, Michelle Fella-Przybylowski, Matthew Gallgher)

Making connections to a curricular model when designing a quality lesson creates a synthesis of essential learning to the content of the course. Maintaining an awareness of Bloom's Taxonomy allows for our planning and preparation to move from a focus of mere skills and knowledge and into more mature and sophisticated means to employ the skills and knowledge taught. The use of technology to project goals and objectives of lessons provides a clarity for students of the learning at hand. A great reflective teaching exercise is to create a powerpoint for a course at the beginning of the school year or semester. For each class, or for each designed lesson, make a slide to state the goals and objectives and other essential information tied to the learning. By the end of the course, a meaningful and reflective digital portfolio is created documenting where the learning started, how it evolved, and how mastery of the fundamental curricular goals and objectives for the course were met. Share this portfolio with systems administrators to evidence rigor and connected learning in your musical classroom.

Thoughtful lesson design leads to higher student engagement, quality ensembles and musical classrooms. When we plan and prepare in meaningful ways, and we share in our teaching portfolio quality lessons that really worked well and why they worked well, we create evidence for systems administrators of why and how we are teaching in rigorous and relevant classroom environments. An extension is to utilize the precious inservice time we have with colleagues in a meaningful way and share out lessons that have worked well for teachers and students. This provides for collegial discussion and sharing of planning and design ideas, as well as the repertoire being used. In conjunction with this, colleagues can also engage in a listening session of literature being rehearsed and performed and/or utilized in a classroom setting.

ASSESSMENT:
A STUDENT'S RESPONSE TO INSTRUCTION

Quality assessing looks like and feels like quality teaching!

Assessment is essential to learning and is a tool and resource for both teachers and students to evidence if goals and objectives are not merely being met, but understood. Quality assessment is learning in action. Students must be given the opportunity to adequately and appropriately learn, via time and instruction, what is intended for mastery. This means assessing for an understanding of essential skills, content and concepts. What seems easy to us may not be for others. Learning occurs in diverse ways. How does our teaching, and thus our assessing, approach the qualitative methods of learning skills, content and concepts if the end result is for students to "get it?" To understand the learning at hand? And how do we respond when they don't get it? Quality assessment is rooted in timely and specific feedback and develops naturally from classroom instruction. The ideal is to thread together instruction and assessment to align our instructional goals, state and national standards, and essential curricular content. Assessment supports instruction by allowing for students to demonstrate skills and knowledge in a *directly observable* fashion. Assessment is a student's response to instruction.

In the book *Natural Classroom Assessment: Designing Seamless Instruction and Assessment* by Smith, Smith and DeLisi, the following points are the foundations to their ideals:

- Good assessment begins with instructional goals and actual instruction.
- An assessment can be a quality natural assessment because it looks like instruction.
- Assessment that facilitates the teaching and learning process in the classroom is the key.
- A justification or rationale for assessing is based in the degree to which it enhances the achievement of the instructional goals and objectives.
- Quality assessment provides students with the opportunity to show what they know and can do.

The authors state, "The superficial coverage of a wide variety of objectives is usually not as helpful to students as thorough coverage of fewer objectives." In other words, be specific. Less is more. Choose quality over quantity.

In designing quality assessment, the authors state two corollary questions which should be answered when planning for assessment:

- What do I want students to be able to know, understand and do?
- What have we been doing instructionally to learn the content/concepts/skills?

Defining the relationship between the assessment evidence and the instructional goals assists in determining the content of the assessment and what evidence we are soliciting (the *how*). Question one also defines what it is we want students to do for the assessment to show evidence (the *what*). Question two secures that the relationship of the assessment and instructional goals reflect what is occurring in the classroom.

The key is in the planning, preparation and design of goals and objectives. As instructional goals become more interesting, more challenging, and more useful to students, so too do assessments. Quality assessments should include clear directions, clear expectations, fairness, and respect. As Smith,

Smith, and DeLisi state, "If you tell students what you want, you are more likely to get it." (p. 51) There are multiple measures and modes of assessment to consider, but the key is to make certain the assessment is an extension of learning.

Assessment occurs before, during and after learning. When introducing new content, we should ask ourselves, in our planning stages, if there are prerequisite skills or knowledge needed by students to learn and understand the "new" learning at hand. How do we assess, in our planning and deployment of our teaching, whether students have this prerequisite knowledge? During learning, assessments are formative in nature. They can be planned or unplanned ways in which we check for understanding.

Culminating assessments, or summative assessments, can be diverse in their format. The key is to match the type of assessment to the learning goals students are to make evident. An important consideration is that after assessment, we need to identify learning gaps and how we might re-teach or approach learning to support students who did not get it. It is essential to reflect upon how foundational musical skills and knowledge grow, evolve, mature and become more sophisticated, and to make these connections with our students. When teachers and students are aware of where learning is on the continuum, and quality assessment is deployed, all stakeholders in the learning process can move musical learning forward in a meaningful way.

ADDITIONAL RESEARCHERS AND RESOURCES

The aforementioned individuals, organizations and models are resources vital to supporting music education. Keep active in the world of education beyond music and draw connections with current educational research to your classroom. ASCD (formerly known as the Association for Supervision and Curriculum Development) is one stop shopping when it comes to locating quality materials from these individuals and organizations. Other researchers/ authors like Carol Ann Tomlinson, Doug Reeves, Fischer and Frey, Heidi Hayes Jacobs, Yong Zhao and many others are essential components of professional growth and understanding. It is important for us to understand how these fundamentally "educational" initiatives and individuals connect with music, and for us to be the musicians making the connections through these lenses to our educational classrooms.

Beyond educational researchers, relevant writers on subjects dealing with influences upon music as well as business models and writings on leadership support us in our vision to grow music education (authors such as Jim Collins, Ken Robinson, Malcolm Gladwell, Daniel Levitin, Howard Gardner, Daniel Coyle, Richard Florida, and Daniel Pink). Another group of writers are those who engage us in the affective and musical realm of education. James Jordan's series which begins with *The Musician's Soul* and

Parker Palmer's *The Courage to Teach* are examples. Authors such as Edward S. Lisk, Dr. Tim Lautzenheiser, and Dr. Larry Blocher provide a treasure of study and immersion into the pedagogical and methodological aspects of music. To evolve as musical teaching professionals there is much for us to study and learn. The only limiting factor is ourselves and the parameters we place on what we do and why we do it.

Within the auspices of effective organizational aspects, essential components for developing a comprehensive music education program in an educational environment can be charted.

The following list identifies critical components to know and understand in music education programs. While we may not have direct control over all components listed, it is important to understand the process and protocol for each. These components contribute to the rigor, relevancy, sustainment and growth of the music education programs within a larger school system.

—Components of a Comprehensive Music Education Program—

- Budget
- Facilities and Technology
- Professional Development
- Recruitment and Retention
- Data Collection and Analysis
- Scheduling and Staffing
- Extra-curricular Programs
- Systems Integration
- Program Curricular Design

These components are broken out into different domains for the purpose of organization and explanation, but everything works together for the benefit of developing, sustaining, and growing an exceptional music education program for the benefit of the students in the system. Each compliments and impacts the others. None work effectively in isolation. A symbiotic relationship between all components promotes a comprehensive music education program.

BUDGET

Definition: The monetary funds needed to support the essential components of the music education program.

Identification: What are the essential components of the music education program that need to be budgeted for annually? What are the larger investment items that need to be budgeted for either (1) over stages/years or (2) every three, four, or five years?

Examples:

Annual: Sheet music, supplies, a repair budget, dry cleaning of uniforms, maintenance items, stands, chairs, instruments, professional development

Non-annual: software and hardware upgrades, large instrument purchases, uniforms, risers and furniture, music and instrument storage systems.

Budget implications are foundational to all facets of the music education program. It impacts staffing, scheduling, facilities, resources and materials, professional development, and the design of curricular and extra-curricular opportunities for students. The ways in which systems budget for programs are diverse, and so the prompts below are to help music education program leaders think about the resources and allocation of funds essential to music, and how to substantiate the funding requests.

Questions for Consideration:
The "Do You Knows" about Your System

- Is the budget process school based or system based?
- Is there a music education supervisor or liaison who supports the system-wide budgeting process?
- Does the department work together or in isolation in preparing the budget?
- How are funds dispersed to schools and what is allocated in each school's budget?
- If in a system with multiple schools of the same grade bands, how is budgeting determined?
- Do teachers in all elementary schools who teach the same genre have access to equitable funds for materials, supplies and resources?
- Do teachers in all middle schools who teach the same genre have access to equitable funds for materials, supplies, and resources?
- Do teachers in all high schools schools who teach the same genre have access to equitable funds for materials, supplies, and resources?
- Does the budget equitably meet the needs of students in all schools within the system?
- Is there an existing inventory of the music-related items in each school (for example stands, chairs, instruments, supplies, and sheet music)? This helps answer the questions: what do we have, what do we need, are students in music education being served equitably, and how can we meet the needs of (a) our program and (b) our students?

- Are there schools with socioeconomic needs which garner more
  or additional resources and support so that all students in the
  system have access to music?

These are important questions to ask when working for the benefit of the whole.

FACILITIES AND TECHNOLOGY

Definitions:

Facilities encompasses everything in regard to the structure of the classroom, performance venues (indoor and outdoor), and the aesthetics which support the functionality of the classrooms and performances spaces.

Identification: large instrumental and vocal classrooms, general music classrooms, music technology labs, practice rooms, changing facilities, storage facilities (indoor and outdoor), bathrooms (if you have such a luxury), lighting, electrical, flooring, wall paint/carpet/tile, sound reinforcement for rehearsal, performance spaces, and accoustics.

Technology encompasses the hardware (computers and peripherals) and software applications essential to the curriculum.

Identification: computers, printers, external drives and devices, storage for student work, software, software upgrade schedule, supplies (printer toner, paper, diverse cabling), auxiliary lab instruments (keyboards, electronic drums), workstations and furniture, lab environment systems.

Facilities is another factor which is as diverse as the buildings in the school district. But conditions of facilities are an essential ingredient for establishing a conducive learning environment. Addressing facility needs goes beyond the physical space, as the aesthetics of the space are equally as important as the space itself. Other factors such as appropriate levels of lighting, maneuverability of the space, storage, and safety all contribute to a quality musical environment. I am not saying that every classroom has to be the Taj Majal, but space and the factors that support quality learning must be reflected upon and an improvement plan must be designed. The existence of disrepair or exhibition of potential safety factors must be addressed.

Charlotte Danielson's four domains of professional practice address classroom environment. Facilities are a contributing factor to how all else evolves and contributes to the quality of learning delivered in our programs. Facilities literally set the stage for learning. When we plan and prepare for our classes, do we have adequate space to execute the lessons we plan? Do we have the space, lighting, support structures, and the equipment to deliver quality instruction? Both of these questions evolve from the environmental conditions which are naturally generated through the external factors imposed upon our teaching and the means by which classroom environment supports musical learning. As music teachers we are very resourceful and we will literally teach anywhere. We all have taught in classrooms, hallways, auditoriums, closets turned into practice rooms, and even in the janitor's office (hopefully when not being used). Many general music teachers are now on carts, toting around their worldly musical possessions so that music remains a component of many overcrowded schools where art and music classrooms have been overtaken for other genre. If a teacher is assessed through the four domains of professional practice (for example, currently in Pennsylvania the domains are the structure for how teachers receive their annual evaluations), is it an equitable expectation that a teacher who has to import him or herself into another person's space is evaluated similarly as the person who lives in the classroom? We tend to put learning and music first, but we often settle for any circumstance which we can mold into a makeshift classroom. We are able to look beyond the environment, but it is imperative to the legitimacy of our programs that we have equitable and appropriate space for our instructional delivery.

Assessment of teaching through classroom environment goes well beyond the physical structure of the rooms, and it also gauges the atmosphere the teacher creates for learning. But a standard should be established within the system to (1) study the equitable space allocation for music education programs and (2) study the conditions of the music facilities throughout the system so that a needs assessment can be developed and deployed (if needed). Having a plan is critical. It is important that when we share data with system administrators that we also come prepared with a plan which explicitly details how to make improvements and why they are essential. As the music educator, we will much prefer to design the plan, solicit information from quality vendors who make and install music-specific components, and to submit this proposal. Obviously, aesthetic needs like fresh paint, carpet, tile, caulking—whatever can be forecasted by the facilities management team in the system—can be remedied through this office. But specifics to music education must be investigated and proposed by the music educator who knows the true needs and quality of what must become a component of the classroom. Be willing to work with system administrators, and to develop a three- or five-year plan for those facilities items which you feel must be tended to. Here is an example. A middle school instrumental music room had serious storage issues. The overcrowding and lack of space for storage resulted in many instruments just sitting on the floor in the back of the room. This posed serious safety issues for both the instruments and the students. The teachers knew that they could never request to have the concrete risers in the room destroyed and a flat concrete floor laid. While this would have significantly increased the space in the classroom and the management of hundreds of instruments both school and student owned, the conclusion was to investigate installing new instrument storage cabinets. They needed to get a quote to replace all of the falling down wooden shelves and to make a four-year plan which was presented to their administration. In the plan they detailed the specifics of the vendor and the types of cabinets needed based upon annual student enrollment by instrument and through the inventory of school owned instruments. The teachers contacted several vendors and decided upon the company that best suited their needs, both in price and quality. In addition to bringing specs and every facet of information from the vendor about the cabinets to the administration, they detailed the four-year cycle for the purchase and installment of the cabinets. This way, as the professional musician-educators, they systemically decided upon cabinet implementation that would not be a distraction to the program. The cabinet installation would become a quality investment which supported it. In a well planned and articulated presentation to administration, the plan was approved. Why? They did their homework and came prepared.

The same process can be utilized to propose the establishment of a middle school music technology program. A school district was successful in establishing one music technology lab in one school. The teachers developed a carefully detailed plan of technological specifics, cost, and learning benefits to students. Items like the electrical wiring and painting were itemized, but these details could be provided (and thus budgeted for by facilities). They provided the specifics in terms of hardware (not the actual computers—this role was fulfilled by the technology department, which budgets for computers—the teachers gave the minimum specifications for the computer systems needed to effectively use the software being proposed and then asked that the technology experts in the system make the best match in regard to computers for the lab). The specifics of software programs, piano keyboards, and communication systems rendering the lab "silent"—and thus not inhibiting or interrupting other classes—were also detailed in the plan. Additional peripherals were itemized and, if music specific, cost forecast was a projection made in working with vendors.

The bottom line is to understand your role as music educator in your communication of space needs and essentials which support the quality of your program. Then, come with a solution and be resourceful. Provide the information specific to music, and work with your facilities and technology departments to provide their insight in the areas where they are the experts.

The effective "pilot" of the middle school music technology went beyond the request and building of the lab. Once installed, teaching in the lab had to be effective and inspiring so that students would want to be immersed in the lab environment. This was evidenced through public relations campaigns and student involvement data. Teachers made the case that labs should be deployed in the other two middle schools based upon their successful planning and deployment of the first lab. They began teaching in the lab as much as possible, and organized lunch time sessions when students could get a pass after lunch to come and create music in the lab. After these sessions became booked, teachers opened the lab every morning 30 minutes before the start of school so students could come in and create. They got involved in the district level technology fair each year to show the community what students were creating and learning in the lab. Finally, the music faculty contacted the local newspaper about their unique lab and they sent a reporter out who did a full story with pictures on what was happening in the middle school lab. They were certain to document and collect all of this positive feedback so that when it was time to go back to system administration and "make the case" for the other two middle schools to install music technology labs, the worth and value of what students were learning and producing was evident to all stakeholders and decision makers. Another lesson learned was in starting small. They figured out what worked well in the first lab and what didn't. In the subsequent two installations, improvements in design and deployment of the lab were addressed and made.

As a music education teacher-leader, your collaborative efforts with systems administration, beyond your building principal, is essential. These teachers were able to build a strong collaborative relationship with the director of technology, and this helped to move the program forward to serve the technologically driven students in a rigorous, relevant, and musically creative way.

**Questions about Facilities that Are Worth Exploring
for the Benefit of Your Programs,
But More Importantly for the Benefit of Your Students:**

- Has an inventory of all teaching spaces for music education in each building in the system been completed and compiled in one clear document?

- Has a needs assessment of teaching spaces been completed and have plans been designed to support the classrooms of music educators in your system?

- Are facilities, while perhaps looking different, consistent in regard to space and size through the schools to support instructional delivery?

- Are the emerging technology needs of music education classrooms studied and planned for accordingly?

- Is there a planned rotation for renewal of subscriptions and/ or system-wide/school site licenses for essential software music educators utilize in their school district?

- Is the hardware up to date and can it support the specifications of the software?

- Is there a computer replacement schedule that musician education program leaders are aware of? Take responsibility to keep the schedule on task!

It is essential to have a positive rapport and relationship with the facilities and technology teams in the system. Inform them of your ideas, be willing to collaborate, and to work together for the common cause of supporting education. If we become roadblocks, so too will our systems, and support for our programs will be diminished. Know and understand the system protocol. Begin any project plan by informing the appropriate personnel and keeping communication open and positive.

Professional Development

Definition: The means by which teachers grow and learn to expand upon their pedagogical, methodological, and teaching skills.

Identification: personal professional growth goals, content specific sessions, graduate programs and graduate credit sessions, system inservice, and departmental/program clinics.

Teaching is an art form which grows and matures through time. In our personal professional growth as we refine our skills and delivery we grow as teachers. However this can not happen in isolation. Quality professional development can occur on many levels. On a local level, it is first the ways in which we reflect upon our own teaching and second, the opportunities provided for us to engage in peer/colleague observations and growth sessions. Critical and respectful discussions about teaching strengths and needs, and personal awareness of where we are and what our improvement goals are are essential in supporting the learning goals of our students. Remember we are there for *them*! It is the maturation and sophistication of ourselves and our teaching abilities, over time, influenced by those we expose ourselves to and the external factors which we immerse ourselves in that supports our growth—and ultimately our students!

The next level of professional development occurs at the building or system level. Quality professional development sessions not only inspire us to want to improve; these sessions provide explicit tools and resources which are relevant to the content that we teach, and are the sessions where we can identify direct connections to the goals of our teaching. I am certain we can all recount varied professional development or inservice sessions which we had to attend in which we sat and either complained to the person next to us or zoned out trying to figure out how in the world this talk on blah blah blah has any relevant connection to what we teach and thus do on a daily basis.

So find a solution. Propose for an upcoming professional day a plan which is content-specific. If funds are in short supply, work together to provide peer sessions on quality teaching strategies. Be resourceful. Find the funds or work with a vendor or company to support getting that specific individual or organization you feel will support the professional growth of your faculty to your teachers—whatever it takes!

The third way to seek opportunities for professional growth are through graduate studies and/or programs run by various organizations (whether for credit or not). Teachers are typically in one of three situations in regards to outside professional development.

1. As a beginning teacher recently certified and needing to accumulate the credits to move from a provisional teaching certificate to a permanent certificate. This may or may not be tied to coursework which is granted through graduate credit, and your system may or may not reimburse the funds needed for attending courses of this nature. Some systems require, beyond the state criteria, matriculation into a graduate program in order to receive reimbursement for tuition. The bottom line is that there is an expectation of completion of this professional development.

2. The next situation is the mid-career teacher who has completed the criteria for permanent certification but can still advance his/her salary by additional coursework. These courses may not have to be part of a prescribed program, but reimbursement for tuition may still be available.

3. The last group is veteran teachers who have earned a post-baccalaureate degree, and have taken the necessary coursework to advance to the upper echelon of the salary scale. However, the state may have a system of accounting for professional growth in place in which a period of time is designated and either hours or credits of time must be completed. Teachers can accrue the hours through inservice time, professional development opportunities hosted by the system, or through outside coursework, workshops, or seminars.

For all groups, the bottom line is that professional growth supports teaching and the learning in our classroom communities. Teaching is an art form which adapts with current educational trends. We must be flexible and open to growth and new resources. We must make sure we are on the cusp of the educational evolution, so that our programs can move forward and evolve with education and the larger implications and initiatives set forth.

Some Professional Development Questions for Consideration:

If the system wants us at our best, the system needs to support us growing into our potential.

*   Is there a professional development plan for the music education program?
*   Has a vision for the needs of music teachers and their areas of growth been identified so that training can be developed?
*   Who will lead the way in organizing these efforts and communicating the professional growth needs of the program?

RECRUITMENT, RETENTION AND DATA: TEACHER-LEADERS IN ACTION

Definitions:

Recruitment: The measures we take to engage students in our music education programs which are elective in nature or involve choice in participation.

Retention: The measures we take to keep students involved in our music education programs which are elective in nature or involve choice in participation.

Identification: Performance ensembles originating in band, chorus, and orchestra: jazz band and jazz vocal ensembles, chamber ensembles both vocal and instrumental, small ensembles, marching band, indoor guard and percussion, and alternative ensembles.

Recruitment and Retention is a critical initiative. In the systems I grew up with and then taught in, music was learning everyone received typically through the eighth grade. At the elementary level, all students were scheduled for general music class. In middle school we had a choice of band/chorus/orchestra/general music, but one of the four was a mandatory component of our education. As the educational times change, and with each state having its own requirements, the ways in which music is mandated and scheduled is diverse. Reflect upon your personal experiences as student and teacher and think about when music was mandated and when music became a choice.

For many elementary school-aged students, choice begins in the form of beginning instrumental music, or being involved with chorus, chimes choirs, musicals, handbells, and other types of ensembles which support the elementary school community and the interests of the students.

Recruitment begins in elementary school. Often children choose one of these additional music opportunities because they have an older sibling involved, a family member may be a musician, the recruitment assembly sparked their interest, or they enjoy listening to music and simply have a curiosity they wish to pursue—or some combination of all above, or for a completely different reason. Once students are immersed in this new program, retention kicks in; the "how do we keep them engaged?" and more importantly "how do we extend to them the beauty of music so that they continue because they too are passionate about this art form?" are answered.

Recruitment certainly continues at all levels and grade bands, and the deployment of recruitment is determined by the established music education program in the system. Retention is what occurs once students have entered the music education program and we encourage the continued participation in our ensembles and musical classrooms. There are two main components to retention: (1) students electing to continue in an ensemble when music moves from being a mandatory subject to an elected one, and (2) when students make a building change (for example, elementary to middle school, middle school to high school). Data is a powerful tool for helping us understand the sustenance of our music education programs, and data can help us to pinpoint breakdowns and/or inconsistencies in recruitment and retention. Annual data collection of program participation is an essential tool. Identification of critical issues or areas of breakdown in program participation can be addressed. Data allows for system administrators to readily view objective data of the number of students involved as active musicians in the system community.

DATA COLLECTION AND ANALYSIS

Definition: The annual and consistent compilation of student information and the analysis of the data which directly impacts the music education program.

Identification: Data which address the number of students per grade, per school, per level involved in music. Data which identify the number of students by instrumentation or voice involved in music. The number of ensembles, and the identification of all ensembles, curricular and extra-curricular in the system. The correlation of system proficiency data for all students involved in the music program (typically collected and assessed by the teacher responsible for the individuals in his/her ensemble(s)). The analysis of all data listed above which results in a systems-wide report to support and substantiate the value of music throughout the system.

Before I share my take on this component I must say this—and it is not a commercial, it is honest quality reading. Purchase Edward S. Lisk's book *The Creative Director: Conductor, Teacher, Leader* and read his chapter on leadership. This is where all of my planning and design evolved from, and it is a quality model which is rooted in his experiences as a program leader in the Oswego City School District in New York where he established an exemplary model program.

Annual data collection should be an initiative that music program leaders develop and building-level music educators understand and value. As an example, data collection can be designed in the following way:

1. Every music educator in the system is given a spreadsheet where they will record, for all elected courses and ensembles, the numbers of students involved. These spreadsheets should be broken down into specific components so that data can be further disaggregated. For example, templates are created for band, chorus, and orchestra by instrumentation/voice vertically, and by grade band horizontally. Teachers can compile their individual totals and report out on the percentage of students in that school participating in his/her ensemble. If there are multiple teachers in one school, they can combine their data to get a true indication of the total number of students involved in the musical community of that building.

2. By an established date, teachers report back to the data collection leader. The role of data collector is to compile information for all schools within the system, and this data is entered onto a master spreadsheet by template (band, chorus, orchestra, and all other ensembles). On an entry level, this will indicate the ensembles at each school and the percentage of students in each building in the system participating.

3. On a larger scale, the data collector can then compile grade band percentages (for example, percent of elementary school participation or high school participation) and the total percent of students within the system involved in the musical community.

4. The preparation and presentation of this compiled information—first to the teachers in the program and then to system administrators—is critical feedback. When data by genre and by grade are collected, teachers can draw conclusions and plans for improved design. Effective strategic

management of recruitment initiatives, or how to bridge the gap between building changes, if a drop in enrollment is seen due to an environmental change, can also be activated.

In my personal experiences as a middle school band director and music supervisor, this information is highly valuable. As a department, we were able to address recruitment and retention issues, and we designed better communication and collaboration between building changes to support students in their questions and concerns about new schools and musical environments. When we compiled district-wide data exhibiting the number of students involved in music throughout our community, administrators understood the value of our programs when they learned about the extent to which students elected to participate in our ensembles.

I would like to take this opportunity to discuss data from one other perspective and this is in regard to student proficiency. With the inception of *No Child Left Behind* and the reauthorization of ESEA (still pending and ever evolving as of this writing), as teaching professionals we understand the continued importance for students to perform at or beyond proficiency on state exams. The added pressure for classroom teachers to prepare students, and the efforts through intervention strategies to close the achievement and opportunity gaps, leaves musician-educators in a very complex position. I use the word *complex* because all teachers are feeling stretched in one way or another. But the complexity for music educators is the means by which we communicate with teachers and system administrators to support the value of musical learning. The positive impacts of our learning environments should support proficiency, and we can identify this quality in our programs by studying system level proficiency data.

This is a story about the power of proficiency data and how misconceptions about pull-out lesson programs were proven wrong. One year, a second year strings teacher was encountering difficulties in scheduling his students for pull-out lessons. Classroom teachers were concerned that pulling the students out of essential class time was hindering their learning and posing potential proficiency pitfalls. He met with the teachers and the administrator to discuss scheduling, but there was little collaborative collegiality. They simply could not work the issue out. The building principal contacted the supervisor responsible for the music program to help mediate a resolution to the situation. The supervisor went to the district data manager and asked if teachers have access to the proficiency scores of their students and was informed that every teacher in the district has access to student proficiency data. She had no idea, and surely none of the music teachers knew this either. So she learned the system, which was web-based and could be accessed by any teacher at school or at home. She learned how to create groups so they could analyze the string teacher's student population. She made an appointment to sit down with the strings teacher to study the proficiency data. The result? All of the students in the string program at this school were proficient, and the overwhelming majority were in the advanced category, scoring highest among students of their age range in the state. They compiled the information and met with the school administrator, who was equally surprised at the data. The issue of missing classroom time for pull-out lessons became a non-issue. In fact, they substantiated why the pull-out lessons actually made the students more responsible school citizens as they had to manage their time efficiently and effectively, and be accountable for time missed in their primary classroom. The supervisor and the strings teacher met with the fifth grade teachers and the real issue was identified. It was an inconvenience for the classroom teachers to have students coming and going from their classrooms. It was not that the students were suffering academically due to the pull-out lesson schedule.

What did the music teachers do at the next elementary grade band inservice? They scheduled a half day in a computer lab and learned how to pull the proficiency data for their ensemble students, how to generate proficiency reports for their students individually and as a composite, and they reported back to their building administrators on their findings. Eventually the entire music education department was inserviced in this way, and this set another precedent, using the system level data to support *why* music is essential and not merely special.

The study of data in diverse ways must happen annually. Data are direct evidence, in systems language, that concretely and objectively shows the positive impacts that music education has upon students engaged in our learning environments.

Recruitment, Retention, and Data-Based Questions for Consideration:

- How does the department address recruitment and retention?
- Is there an annual study?
- And to what extent and means is data analyzed?
- Is there a music education program data team?
- A designated data collector leader?
- Or a systematized means by which data is collected, studied, analyzed, and then reported on?
- Do music educators in the system know the ways in which they can utilize systems data in support of their programs?

SCHEDULING AND STAFFING

Definitions:

Scheduling: The matrix developed for the deployment of music education classes throughout a system.

Identification: Horizontal equity to support curriculum delivery in schools within the system of the same grade bands, vertical equity to support the articulation of the curriculum through the grade bands of the system, and appropriate course lengths (both in minutes per period and days per school year) which support the learning and maturation of students in music education courses and ensembles.

Definitions:

Staffing: The appropriate and reasonable number of teachers hired to support the learning needs of students and the curricular content established within the program. Additional adjunct staff may be hired for additional support positions with extra-curricular ensembles.

Identification: Instrumental and vocal specialists trained and certified in music education who share the ideals of the music education program philosophy and who will work as collaborative members of the program for the benefit of student learning and musicianship.

One of the biggest impediments to music education today is the scheduling process. It is one of the most inconsistent aspects of our systems, and one of the most neglected for musical needs unless we have a supportive administrator or we have taught the scheduler how to schedule music. We must teach beyond our classrooms! Our biggest obstacle in delivering a quality music education program is finding the time to do so. While the school day in most places remains in the same time structure, each year it seems that more and more measures are deployed within this set number of minutes per day. What this results in is "more is less." All essentialists (replaces the word *specialists*) are vying for time. What we must make certain is that music does not become a convenience. Time must remain a necessity.

In the February 1, 2011 online edition of Education Week, in the article *The Skills Connection Between the Arts and 21st Century Learning*, author Bruce D. Taylor writes, "The cumulative amount of instructional time an elementary music teacher has in the school year is approximately 32 hours. This is less than the equivalent of a standard workweek to produce two concerts with 200 or more kids. Given this time constraint, perhaps all that can be accomplished is replication—not learning, much less understanding." He goes on to state, "I propose that the critical skills of creativity, critical thinking, and problem-solving can be developed by design—not acquired by accident or as a byproduct—using the arts as tools...Why am I convinced that this would work? Because the arts relate to the unique ways in which human beings think."

In the 21st Century Skills Framework, there are six learning and innovation skills which are identified as essential to learning: (1) creativity, (2) innovation, (3) critical thinking, (4) problem solving, (5) communication, and (6) collaboration. Let's be a model for our students and work together to systematically establish priorities for the benefit of our students. When we substantiate through data the number of students involved in our music education programs—and we utilize this evidence to indicate why music is essential—then we are professionals prepared to communicate and collaborate with administrators to support the musical education of our students.

If we are asking our students to learn and understand these six essential skills, let's be a model for how to actively use these skills for their benefit. The means by which we communicate the needs of our program and the essential learning environments which all teachers deserve lead to a creative collaboration to work towards equitable and reasonable scheduling.

Seeing students for 20 days a year for music class is not the answer. Engaging students for one marking period out of four in a year for music class is not the answer. If a student has 7th grade general music during the first semester of that year and then the fourth semester of his 8th grade year, how can we possibly legitimize learning retention through a rigorous and relevant curriculum? This student, and many out in the real world, face this situation every year. How is a student expected to recall 1.5 years later what was learned at the beginning of his 7th grade year? Poor scheduling is a result of inaction and complacency and identification of a better plan. Poor scheduling can be a result of trying to fit too much into the current structure and time frame, resulting in a less-is-not-more approach. In recent years, middle school schedules have become overloaded creating diverse experiential opportunities for students, lacking depth and breadth of content. Every day for a marking period courses, and courses on vectors splitting the year into five compartments of about 20 days a course, are now common. Poor scheduling compromises learning. If we are not willing to be honest and work through the tough roadblocks, to be leaders in our systems for the benefit of our students, then we have no choice but to settle for minimum standards and disengaged classrooms. Some of these situations are beyond our control, but awareness of the ineffectiveness must be made evident. The effective organization components are interrelated, and each aspect of this program design model supports the sustenance and growth of the whole.

The Dr. Tim mantra:
**"If you continue to do what you have always done,
you will continue to get what you have always gotten."**

Scheduling Questions to Consider:

- Do music education leaders in the district meet with appropriate administrators to support equitable scheduling and the needs of students who choose music?
- Is staffing equitable across the system? How do you know this? The answer is in the data!

Are there impediments in scheduling which impact the availability of music classes for students? If so, how do we solve these issues? Are we going to do what we have always done? Or are we going to choose to lead? Let's move out of the *if only* state and into the empowerment mode to creatively improve upon existing and identified roadblocks to learning. Create a vision for the future! New ideas! New forms! Go!

Extra-Curricular Ensembles, Music Organizations and Other Affiliations

Definition: The ensembles which meet outside of the school day supporting the curricular program and providing an extension of musical learning and immersion for students.

Identification: Jazz band, marching band, color guard, pit orchestra, musical, chamber singers, women's chorus, men's chorus, jazz vocal ensemble, chamber ensembles both instrumental and vocal, string quartets, indoor percussion and color guard, music technology club, student audio, production and lighting engineers, small ensembles both instrumental and vocal, rock bands, fusion ensembles, stage bands, bucket drumming ensembles, handbells and chimes ensembles, laptop and electronic ensembles...and everything else you have creatively provided for your students!

I am a firm believer that our primary investment must be to the curricular program. When students invest their in-school time to music, they are learning the foundational studies which support all extensions and involvements in music outside of school. When students realize the worth and value of the curricular program, and they feel that we, as teachers, are investing time in something we are passionate about and which we believe in, they will form opinions and make decisions as to how to commit their time outside of the school day to music. Honestly, these choices are most often made because 1) they enjoy music and want to be immersed more, 2) students understand and value the meaning of the musical learning, and 3) the teacher(s) inspire(s) them to become more involved and to evolve their love of music. Often they choose music because they choose us.

Extra-curricular ensembles are often those which are most evident in the community by the nature of the purpose they may serve. The most obvious example of this is marching band. Whether it is on Friday night at the weekly football game, or marching down main street in the annual parade, the ways in which the community observes the ensembles which interact with it often determine the necessary support to sustain our programs. This is the honest truth. It is important to share our student's musicianship with the community and to actively engage in reaching out to all populations who reside in our systems, whether this be taking some small chamber ensembles to perform at a local retirement community, forming an intergenerational choral experience, or visiting a local day care with a small brass ensemble to perform for students. The means by which we utilize our extra-curricular ensembles to support our curricular program are vital choices we make.

However, in a system serving several towns and/or communities, it is important for music program leaders to have a firm grasp of all performing ensembles at all levels and grade bands, both curricular and extra-curricular and to take account of how these ensembles serve not only the students but also the community. I am not saying that every school has to do exactly the same things, but equity and continuity speak volumes throughout a system, and students from all corners of the system should have similar opportunities that other schools within the system employ and enjoy.

When a system music education program assesses all components of how the music program is serving students, equity has many faces. Extra-curricular opportunities are essential components to nurturing our students, and they must work to serve the students well in these diverse buildings.

Extra-curricular ensembles can also function as great communication and promotion tools for recruitment and retention. Think of hosting side by side concerts for students making a building change the following year. Invite students to the school community they will be moving into to spend a day of music-making with the students in the building. Make time to speak with prospective students, and for the students to work with you in an ensemble setting. Send a small jazz combo down to elementary recruitment day and have them play for the students. Bring the high school chorus to the middle school and make the experience a real one for these up and coming students.

Encourage eligible students to audition for community groups, and regional and/or state music education association ensembles. Provide your students with the ideas and the encouragement to experience music in school and beyond.

The possibilities are endless, and the choice...is yours.

Some Extra-Curricular Questions for Consideration:

- Are there consistent and equitable extra-curricular opportunities for students across the system?
- How do we know?
- Is this data collected annually?
- Specifically, where several schools of the same grade bands are existent within the system, are there ensembles which reach all students and share a common thread?
- Are extra-curricular ensembles funded equitably through the system?
- Is there a support system in place?
- Is there an opportunity for teachers to meet and dialogue about the ensembles in their schools or the ones they wish to start?
- Are there professional development opportunities to support teachers in their growth for extra-curricular purposes?

Systems Integration and Program Curricular Design

Everyone would like to be the best, but most organizations lack the discipline to figure out with egoless clarity what they can be the best at and the will to do whatever it takes to turn the potential into reality.

—*Jim Collins,* Good to Great *(p.128)*

We have a 'strategic' plan. It's called doing things.

—*Herb Kelleher, founder, Southwest Airlines*

In Ken Robinson's book, *The Element,* he says, "education is the system that's supposed to develop our natural abilities and enable us to make our way in the world." (p. 16) The essential ingredients for success in any educational arena are the systems created to support learning. Our systems are standards-based models rooted in key skills and knowledge. But we must think bigger, beyond curriculum and to the system in place called the Music Education Program. This ideal moves us beyond what is learned in a specific genre of music and into collaboration to establish a program-wide vision of the *whats, whys* and *hows* of the musical education the students will receive. This process of identifying a vision for the music education program will allow for efficiency in teaching and learning.

Example:

Many students begin a general music education class in kindergarten. Around the fourth grade our students have the opportunity to begin a band instrument. Students sign up for an instrument and they receive a method book. The method book typically begins with a series of fingerings to learn and whole note/whole rest patterns. Basic vocabulary is established: whole note, whole rest, staff, measure, etc. We understand that the intention of the method book is to start a "beginner" instrumentalist with zero prerequisite knowledge. However, for most school systems where general music began four years earlier, hasn't some of this prerequisite knowledge—and thus the skills to apply this musical knowledge—been established? This is why communication and articulation of curriculum is essential. Students respond to and respect an efficient means of learning. It is our responsibility to communicate and collaborate for the benefit of music education as a *program* in our system. This process requires time and commitment.

There are three stages to creating a unified and cohesive music department program. When detailed in a document which substantiates the whole of the program, outlines the learning benefits to students, and addresses a cohesive plan of action to deploy a meaningful standards-based curriculum thoughtfully, relevance is established. A rigorous and relevant curriculum is articulated both vertically (K through 12, or in some combination thereof, dependent upon the system) and horizontally (communication of benchmarks of musical elements, skills and knowledge through the grades and across musical genre). When a document of this substance is supplied to administrators, it provides a legitimacy of what we teach and thus what students learn through the lens of music. The spirit of this design process follows the Understanding by Design model developed by Grant Wiggins and Jay McTighe. We simply parallel-process some of the ideals of this design model on a program level.

Developing a Collective Vision:

After recalling and perhaps building some prerequisite knowledge about teaching and learning, it is now time to move into the design process. One of the first considerations is who will be on the design team? It is important to include teacher-leaders from diverse musical genres within the system, in diverse career stages, and those with diverse views. Why? While coming to consensus is critical to the process, having honest conversations which challenge our thinking and open our minds to other perspectives is imperative for a healthy and creative process. Often what is found through the design of consensus building is that we might be coming from similar pathways, but our language is different, thus seeming different or askew. The development of the team is the foundation to building vision. Typically teams of 15 to 18 teacher-leaders is appropriate and allows for a myriad of individuals to be involved. However, each system is different and some thinking outside of the box to determine how to process out and design vision and philosophy may take different forms. It is also important that throughout the process, if an entire music education department is not involved, that a sharing out of what is evolving occurs and that colleagues outside of the core team have the opportunity to voice ideas and opinions of the work in progress. This allows for all members of the department to feel some ownership and engagement in the design process.

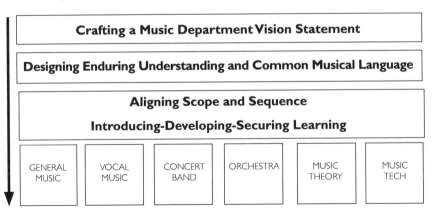

This visual identifies the curricular vision for a cohesive music education program, which delivers a comprehensive music education. It identifies the stages and components of design of the curricular components of a music education program.

Music Education Program Vision Statement:

The initial work for a music education program design team is to draft their collective vision, a philosophical statement of why music is essential in the system. This vision makes evident how music fulfills a significant educational role in the lives of all students. The statement can be understood as a larger in-context *big idea*. The development of enduring understandings support the vision/philosophy. The purpose of the philosophical statement is to encapsulate a collective vision of why the department believes music is essential to education, how music serves student learning, and why music is a vital component of the educational system, community, and beyond. A vision statement should be a malleable document; it should not be static. This vision may change over time. As teaching personnel change and as learning evolves, the document must be allowed to speak as the voice of the music program at all times. One of the challenges of writing a vision statement within a group setting is respecting diverse views, thoughts, and opinions, while identifying the similarities and drives for what we do and why we do it. A process is needed. Individuals must be given the opportunity to express their ideals, as ownership in the vision statement by the music education leadership design team is key.

When teachers are given the opportunity to respond to quality questions which address music education, an objective starting point where threads of cohesion can be discovered is established. The first steps are to write and respond to quality questions regarding the program and to have individuals begin to chart their ideas in a visible means so that connections can be made. Once teachers reflect individually, it is time to report out to the whole.

Identifying key words and phrases through placing check marks next to items which have been identified and statements that others have acknowledged as key components is a way to start. Sculpting a statement in response to each question based upon the feedback of all stakeholders involved in the process begins to solidify the message of the whole. As these singular statements are formed, the means to collectively join them with the other prompts now begins to shape the vision of the department/program.

Some Sample Prompts and Questions:

- Define music in your own words.
- Why is music a valuable and integral component of a student s education and life?
- Who should teach a comprehensive music education program?
- What is the purpose of music education?

I had the opportunity to work through this design process with an extraordinary group of musician-educators in the North Penn School District in Lansdale, Pennsylvania. As the music program is quite large, approximately 15 teachers were engaged in the process and included individuals from diverse musical genres (band, chorus, orchestra, general music, music technology, and music theory), and teachers with diverse years of experience (three years of experience to forty). We utilized this method to go about writing their vision, and I have to say that this experience was one of the most rewarding in my professional career.

This group of musician-educators understands the value of K-12 program articulation. In developing not only a collective vision but an articulated vertical curriculum to substantiate why music education is essential in their school district, they make evident the interconnectedness of teaching in a professional and collegial musical community for the benefit of their students.

Their philosophical statement evolved out of a year-long process of working through a comprehensive program study and design. It reads:

Music is a vital and meaningful component of a child's education and life. It promotes creativity, imaginative and critical thinking, and leads to the development of highly innovative individuals.

Music education provides students with an authentic and unparalleled means of understanding and interacting with the world around them and the person within. Music education cultivates:

- life-long learning
- music appreciation
- self-expression and creativity
- holistic education
- self-discipline and work ethic
- self-worth, awareness and esteem
- collaboration and communication
- interdisciplinary learning
- artistic potential

Music is a natural expression of the human spirit that nourishes the mind, body and soul. Music convenes the emotional, intellectual, physical, aesthetic and social facets of humanity. It activates nearly every area of the brain, engaging students in complex neurological processes.

Music is everywhere: on all continents, in all nations and cultures, in nature, in all segments of society and media. Music transcends time and all of existence as an expression of our intellect and emotions, and as a reflection of our environment.

Developing Enduring Understandings in Support of the Vision Statement:

The development of enduring understandings is essential learning for all students engaged in music education. Enduring understandings, in this process, are established as the support structure to the vision statement. They transcend all musical genres and are established as the overarching musical learnings critical to all students in the system. This is a discrete approach to articulating requisite skills and knowledge, with the ideal that if these are unified across genre, incredible potential in respect to student learning of music through a cohesive curriculum is created.

A process-oriented approach is essential in the identification and writing of enduring understandings. A prompt like: *what should students know and be able to do at the conclusion of this music education program* is a means to begin the process. Programs which work with a smaller grade band may set these benchmarks differently then those larger K-12 systems, where a series of know and be able to do benchmarks at various grade bands may be established. For example: in a K-12 system where all students take music through the 8th grade, and then grades 9-12 music is elective, enduring understandings may first be written as benchmarks at the conclusion of 8th grade. Or benchmarks can be written for the culminating year of each building, before a change to a new grade band (Elementary School - Middle School - High School).

Then, the extension of the learning through grades 9-12 may be identified.

Once enduring understandings are written, skills and knowledge can be identified which concretely support the larger more conceptual goals. This establishes a means by which scope and sequence through courses can be articulated.

Visual Representation of the Connection Between a Vision Statement and Enduring Understandings:

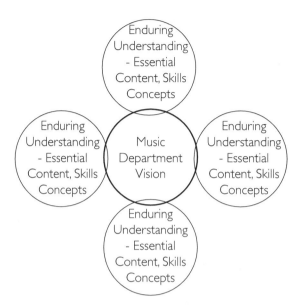

Here are some examples of enduring understandings, supported by skills and knowledge. Note that the National Standards for Music Education and also 21st Century Skills have been relevantly tied to each. These too were written by the music education design team in the North Penn School District. Note the connections of the enduring understandings to the vision statement provided earlier in this section.

As a reference and review, the National Music Education Standards and the 21st Century Skills Framework are first provided.

National Standards for Music Education:

1. Singing, alone and with others, a varied repertoire of music.
2. Performing on instruments, alone and with others, a varied repertoire of music.
3. Improvising melodies, variations, and accompaniments.
4. Composing and arranging music within specified guidelines.
5. Reading and notating music.
6. Listening to, analyzing, and describing music.
7. Evaluating music and music performances.
8. Understanding relationships between music, the other arts, and disciplines outside the arts.
9. Understanding music in relation to history and culture.

21st Century Skills Framework:

21st Century Student Outcomes and Support Systems

Learning and Innovation Skills - 4Cs
Critical thinking • Communication
Collaboration • Creativity

Core Subjects - 3Rs
and 21st Century Themes

Life and
Career Skills

Information,
Media, and
Technology
Skills

Standards
and Assesments

Curriculum and Instruction

Professional Development

Learning Environments

Enduring Understanding 1

Music is a dimension of human expression nurturing creativity by eliciting aesthetic and intellectual responses.

NATIONAL STANDARDS: 6, 7, 8, 9.

21st CENTURY SKILLS: Learning and Innovation Skills, Life and Career Skills

Skills/Content/Concepts:

- To utilize music as a form of communication, self expression, and creativity
- To understand that music affects emotions
- To express thoughts, ideas and emotions through a musical means

Enduring Understanding 2

Music is a language conveying meaning and feeling through the innate ability to understand and interpret the elements of music.

NATIONAL STANDARDS: 1, 2, 3, 4, 5, 6.

21st CENTURY SKILLS: Learning and Innovation Skills

Skills/Content/Concepts:

To hear, speak, read, write, and produce music via established elements

- Melody
- Harmony
- Rhythm
- Form
- Timbre
- Musical Expression

Enduring Understanding 3

Music develops cultural understandings, the appreciation and preservation of history, and promotes global citizenship.

NATIONAL STANDARDS: 8, 9.

21st CENTURY SKILLS: Global awareness, civic literacy, Learning and Innovation Skills, and Life and Career Skills

Skills/Content/Concepts:
- To create an awareness and appreciation of cultural diversity
- To appreciate the historical context and social significance of music
- To develop an appreciation of the scope of music and how it transcends life in all ways
- To cultivate a life long support of the arts
- To recognize quality musical performances through aesthetic and intellectual understandings

ENDURING UNDERSTANDING 4

Music is a complex neurological process activating more areas of the brain simultaneously than any other endeavor, equipping students with a significant advantage for intellectual development.

NATIONAL STANDARDS: 3, 4, 5, 6, 7.

21st CENTURY SKILLS: Learning and Innovation Skills, Life and Career Skills

Skills/Content/Concepts:
- To develop intellectual and creative capacities to their fullest potential
- To utilize musical studies to enhance cognition in all disciplines
- To comprehend and translate linguistic notation into kinesthetic and aural responses
- To create, interpret, listen, improvise and perform music

ENDURING UNDERSTANDING 5

Music is a core subject rigorously preparing the 21st Century Learner with Life and career Skills for an ever-evolving world.

NATIONAL STANDARD: 8.

21st CENTURY SKILLS: Learning and Innovation Skills

Skills/Content/Concepts:
- Creativity and Innovation
- Critical Thinking and Problem Solving Skills
- Communication and Collaboration

Scope and sequence, or mapping of skills and knowledge, allows for the program to tangibly identify the stages of development (introducing - developing - securing) which charts the sophistication and maturation of content and concepts over time in an age and developmentally appropriate means. As benchmarks are established through scope and sequence, learning will increase and deepen. Wiggins states, "We cannot cover concepts and expect them to be understood; we have to uncover or discover their value." (UbD, pg. 46) For example: *Introducing* essential content/skills/concepts in grades kindergarten through three. *Developing* essential content/skills/concepts in grades four through eight. *Securing* essential content/skills/concepts in grades nine through twelve. Once sophistication of knowledge and skills is designed, curricular documents can be studied and revised to synthesize and articulate the program goals and outcomes established through the vision statement, enduring understandings, and scope and sequence. This most local level of curricular design (at the grade/course level), is where skills, content, methodology, and pedagogy utilized, specific to genre, is identified, articulated, and linked to program vision.

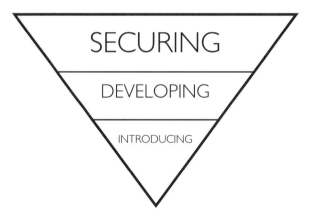

So WHY go through this process? First and foremost, design in this complex, thoughtful, and sophisticated a way is for the purpose of serving students and providing for them a rigorous and relevant musical education. There are three levels of purpose to engaging in program design in this way: (1) to provide the system/district/administration with a cohesive quality model of music education, (2) to bring music education into a collaborative departmental/program environment, and (3) to support the musician-educator, professionally and personally, in growth and maturation through the art of teaching.

For systems and district administrators, program design at this level is a documented blueprint of the music education program. It is viable, as it is written using a sophisticated design tool. It is legitimate, as it is embedded with state and national standards and draws connections to 21ˢᵗ Century learning. It is measurable, via established "evidence" through the scope and sequence of the benchmarks established in support of enduring understandings. It is a reliable document, written by music educators and for music educators, creating ownership of the program.

On the departmental or program level, design in this spirit creates a unified vision of conceptual goals, establishing purposeful teaching and learning. The result is to collectively make musical meaning. Students benefit from the transparency of learning through all musical genre. Creating overarching goals and connecting content tangibly articulates musical growth and development for our musical students.

On the teacher level a means for musician-educators to give to students through what Rick DuFour coins as a loose-tight model is established. The "tight" is: we have identified our program philosophy, goals and expectations with a collective vision. These ideals have been articulated through the curriculum, and the expectation is that teachers will teach to the curriculum. The "loose" is: here are the curricular goals, but I have the autonomy to creatively shape my classroom and to sculpt the learning environment through the design of lessons and the selection of quality repertoire.

Through thoughtful design and collaboration, a map and guide for effective program and lesson design is established. The department has created *purpose*. When the members of that music education faculty are able to pull back and look at the big picture and how the efforts of the teacher at the classroom level are contributing to the goals and ideals established by the department, the vision of creatively teaching to bring musical understanding to all of our students is the result.

So how do we nurture creativity through a musical curriculum, as a teacher, for the benefit of our students? Edward S. Lisk states, "We must teach for understanding and not simply for content." This is evidenced in three ways: by cultivating ownership, inspiring individuals, and making meaning. Effectively establishing our program vision through thoughtful and comprehensive design leads to the opportunity to reflect upon the affective reasons of why music in education is essential in the lives of our students.

.

—PART TWO—

AFFECTIVE LIFELONG POTENTIAL: BRINGING MEANING TO WHY WE MAKE MUSIC

Greatness and nearsightedness are incompatible. Meaningful achievement depends on lifting one's sights and pushing toward the horizon.

—Daniel Pink, Drive

The heart of the melody can never be put down on paper.

—Pablo Casals

The necessity of effective organizational impacts has been identified in regard to how we objectively substantiate and grow our music education programs within a system. However, music does not singularly reside in the discrete skills and knowledge, and neither do we as musician-educators, or the programs through which we bring musical learning to students. Affective lifelong potential provides the "why" of "why music is so meaningful to us." All of these realms of the affective are most accurately the reasons *why* we teach. We did not sign up for this area of teaching because of how much paperwork there is, how hard we have to continually work to substantiate music in education, or the analysis of data in support of our programs. We teach music because music moves us beyond the concrete and into the realm of how it makes us feel, how we develop our expressive and creative self, and how we create purpose, cultivate ownership, and inspire individuals through music every day of our lives. The affective is our *why* we do what we do. Creativity and those skills associated with it in 21st Century learning allow for us to tangibly make evident *why* music is vital in education through the affective domain.

> "Abundance has brought beautiful things to our lives, but that bevy of material goods has not necessarily made us much happier. The paradox is that while living standards have risen steadily decade after decade, personal, family, and life satisfaction haven't budged. That's why more people— liberated by prosperity but not fulfilled by it—are resolving the paradox by searching for meaning." (Pink, A Whole New Mind, p. 35).

Thoughts About Music: Education and Creativity in the 21st Century

In this era of creativity, as the arts are identified as a core component of 21st Century learning for students, musician-educators must take the initiative to clearly define the role that music plays in the lives of students. As we look to the future, we have a responsibility to ensure that our programs are not diminished. We must legitimize the sustenance of what we teach, why we teach, and how a musical education enriches the lives of our students. For the value and integrity of our classrooms to be evident to all stakeholders in the educational spectrum, and to authenticate the evolution of our musical programs, an action oriented plan which dissects the answers to many tough questions is the beginning. We can complain as the frustration builds as we begin to quantify the importance of classes deemed core or non-essential, or we can seek solutions and educate those around us as to the core values of music education in support of the cognitive, emotional, and creative capacities of our students.

Ken Robinson states that we must move out of an industrial model of education which prescribes and manufactures a standardized program of study and move into an agricultural arena, one in which we can cultivate learning based upon the unique qualities of the school and the community of learners.

As musician-educators we have a primary responsibility to foster creativity and to provide learning opportunities which mix content knowledge with intellectual and emotional expression. The musical classroom is one in which students engage in and understand the mind-body-heart connection. The identification of feelings through expressive experiences, and the means by which students learn and discriminate about their inner-self, is distinct to the arts. Music provides opportunities for students to think (mind), feel (heart), while using their bodies (kinesthetically) to produce a highly personal and unique outcome. The role of the teacher is to support human expression that lies within every child, to foster its growth, and to provide an environment which allows students to grow into their own unique humanity.

As the educational stage has changed in many ways, how we nurture creativity and approach learning, teaching, music, and education in the 21st Century is an important contemplation. On the teaching level, creativity threads through our effective organizational impacts and the affective lifelong potential we inspire through our programs. Creativity begins with an idea and initial inspiration in our imagination, which is applied and involves the actions we choose to take or make as musicians and educators. We are creative when we are involved in doing something, and this creative action is applied imagination. Creativity truly becomes innovation when we make imagination and creativity a reality. The question is, what does this look like and feel like in our music education programs?

Ben Zander tags it as being a relentless architect of human potential. As musician-educators we have an immense experiential influence available to our students. It is whether or not we are up for the challenge of giving to our students the potential of beauty that exists within and through living and performing music. Zander states, "I set as the goal the maximum capacity that people have—I settle for no less." Do we approach our musical classrooms in this way? We have before us every day of the school year classes full of students wanting to learn and experience music. Their future is literally in our hands and most often they are electing or choosing our classes. For many students music is why they show up to school every day. In Robinson's 2010

TED Talk he says, "It isn't what you do, it's who you are." To build upon this statement then, the questions are: How much are we willing to give of ourselves? How willing are we to journey with our students to uncover all that music has to offer? In *Organizing Genius* by Warren Bennis and Patricia Ward they state, "The best thing a leader can do for a great group is to allow its members to discover their own greatness." Unlocking the infinite potential living within our students is a choice which begins within ourselves, and is determined by how we perceive our role.

While completing my masters degree in Educational Leadership at St. Joseph's University, I had to take a business of education course. It mainly focused on school code and funding procedures. But our professor, a former superintendent, not only had us learning all of the particulars about Pennsylvania code, he also had us reading articles and books by leading authors in the business industry. At first I did not understand this. I questioned why in an education course we were learning about innovative business practices. How did the two possibly connect? I always thought of business and education as two separate entities. I enjoyed the reading, especially the book *Circle of Innovation* by Tom Peters. It is a study in highly successful businesses who thought and worked outside of the proverbial box and became highly successful as a result. What I learned from this book was that these businesses were focused on the consumer, their experiences, and the goal to satisfy them beyond expectation because of the incredible experience they had through the product or service. With each of the businesses presented in the book the leader was a visionary; someone who was able to look beyond the way things were or are done and to define a new focus and direction instead of re-fining an old practice. These businesses created new forms instead of recreating or attempting to reinvent old forms. This course had my wheels spinning and my curiosity peaked, but I still did not understand the connections between the educational and business worlds and struggled to find connections between them.

Shortly after this course and as I began my work at district office as a learning coordinator, synapses began firing and connections started to be made. This was in large part due to the leadership of our superintendent, Dr. Robert Hassler. For our administrative meetings, he would often have us read a book. I understood the connection to the educational books, but then we were asked to read *Good to Great* by Jim Collins. At that month's administrative meeting he did a presentation about significant components of the book and the connections to our role in how we service and educate students, how we support families, and what our role was in the community. This was a pivotal moment for me as my learnings from my earlier graduate course surfaced and I began to understand and make meaning of these connections. What I was beginning to synthesize, in regard to business and education, began at the district level from the professional development our superintendent provided. Soon, though, I found myself envisioning ways to transform our work at the departmental level. I wanted to dig deeper and so I began my education into authors and understandings written about by Daniel Pink, Richard Florida, Ken Robinson, Malcolm Gladwell, Thomas Friedman, and other notable contemporaries. What I discovered on my reading and reflective journey was that we as a music department needed to have a vision and a mission, a direction, and a plan unlike before. We needed to find new strategies, new ways to inform about why we are essential to the whole of education. The other realization that I made was that we need to cultivate this idea as a collaborative team. The plan became to nurture dynamic leaders, cultivate ownership, make meaning, and to inspire individuals because we understood our purpose and we felt valued in our learning community as musician-educators.

These experiences and the subsequent reading that I did evolved my vision as a leader. The biggest realization that I made was that as a good leader I had to move out of isolation and into creative collaboration with my colleagues. At first this was way out of my type A tendencies—being totally organized, it is easier and more efficient to just do it myself. What I gained from moving beyond my fear and anxiety and into collaboration was the ability to push the creative envelope as we searched for meaning, value, and vision as a collective collegial group; one that was committed to our passion of quality music in education.

EFFECTIVE ORGANIZATIONAL IMPACTS: THROUGH THE AFFECTIVE DOMAIN

If your actions inspire others to dream more, learn more, do more and become more, you are a leader.

—John Quincy Adams

Strong conductor-leaders radiate confidence, which motivates people to believe in themselves and what they can accomplish and achieve. The primary task of a leader is to keep hope alive.

—Frank Battisti, *On Becoming a Conductor*

Leadership is all about love:
Passion, Enthusiasms, Appetite for Life, Engagement, Great Causes & Determination to Make a Damn Difference, Commitment to Excellence, Shared Adventures, Bizarre Failures, Growth Beyond Measure, Insatiable Appetite for Change.

—Tom Peters

LEADERSHIP

A great leader encompasses a particular dynamic and personality, which is not threatening and one which does not threaten. A leader thrives on collaboration and empowering others, in bringing ownership, energy and passion to all involved in the endeavor at hand. The skills of strong leadership must be supported by depth of character, content knowledge, and the ability to look at an organization both globally and intimately; and thus be able to process and act for the common good.

Leadership is never selfish or self-fulfilling. Dynamic leadership is always looking beyond and into the future, creating and growing the vision of what will ultimately bring the most meaning and success to the organization. There must be an inherent degree of inhibition, the ability to be truly *who* you are as a leader, to allow your soul to speak. Authenticity and value in musicianship is essential for the conductor. When abandoned, the ensemble too is dull, lifeless and shallow, void of musical meaning, spirit and connection. Just as a great leader breathes life into an organization or group of individuals, so too does a conductor bring to life the energy of an ensemble.

Leadership cannot be prescriptive or practiced, it must be lived! The creative and imaginative contributions of a conductor-teacher-leader (Edward S. Lisk) fuel innovation, and through new systems employed we find a means of growing—not simply an end product. Effective leadership, and thus meaningful teaching, requires transparency. As a member of an organization or even as a student, one either feels, "Wow, this is going to be great" or "Ugh, here we go again." Haven't we all experienced these situations professionally, personally and musically?

In an email correspondence I shared with Eugene Corporon, I thanked him for taking the time to reply and he wrote the following: "I didn't take time, I invested the time and it was well worth it." When we invest our time as musicians and teachers in our students and the programs that support their learning, there are three ingredients essential for growth; the means by which we cultivate ownership, the ways in which we create purpose by inspiring individuals, and the passion we live through making musical meaning. What drives the time that we invest and our roles as teacher-leaders are the choices we make.

As leaders we need to be highly resourceful; to be creative in overcoming obstacles, in reaching out to parents and our communities so that students may share in the beauty of music. In our day-to-day networking throughout our school buildings with teachers, staff, and administration, we must be attuned to our personal, professional, and program needs. This establishes the highest quality music education standards for our students. The stronger and richer the opportunities, the more tangible rigor and relevance are made evident through learning. Advocacy is a substantial tool for us to utilize, and there is tons of support and research based models to say *why* music. When we show the conclusive and transparent means by which music *is* education, systems administration "get it" because they experience it through the learning environments we create as teacher-leaders.

ADVOCACY THROUGH EVIDENCE:
USING RESEARCH, CURRENT EDUCATIONAL TRENDS,
AND DATA TO SUPPORT MUSIC EDUCATION

The role of data via effective organizational impacts has been made evident, and the story has been shared about the district where proficiency data was used to support the positive facets of a pull-out lesson program. This is one component of a larger whole in regards to how we substantiate our programs. Another component is to utilize the wealth of research and books like *This is Your Brain on Music*, written by Daniel Levitin. This is a wonderful journey through the neurological perspective of the connectivity of cognition and music. As program leaders through, and in keeping in mind the business and innovation authors discussed earlier, an approach to music education support through tangible evidence of our programs in our home districts, of what they are, who they service, and the impacts of the learning in our classrooms is another approach to creative and collaborative leadership to organize and materialize what it is we do. The truth of the matter is that most administrators do not have an understanding of our programs, our curriculum, or what quality teaching and learning in our musical classrooms looks and feels like simply because most administrators are not musician-educators and their prior experiences as a student and learner through music may have been positive or negative. Often we do not know. Have you ever asked an administrator what his/her experience was with music as a child in school? There is the chance that bias has been created due to a former personal experience. Or maybe they have a child of their own who is currently involved in music. Make a personal connection. Uncover if there is a relationship with music that your administrator might have and cultivate it for better or for worse. It is our job to teach and to educate on a local level the value and meaning our classrooms bring to the larger educational whole of our systems of learning. Our goal is to inform and to show the value of our programs; to change minds and hearts through quality music making.

This ideal then suggests the establishment of a few critical masses: (1) a collaborative group of teacher-leaders who are committed to putting an action plan in process, (2) a shift of paradigm in regard to how we advocate, and (3) the deployment of a plan which uncovers data about our programs and has the courage to discuss and mediate tough challenges through honesty and integrity.

It is acknowledged that many of our school systems have become data driven organizations which utilize evidence to make educational decisions. Evidence is tangible, objective, real-time accountability of what we do, who we involve, and how they perform in our classrooms and beyond. Assessment is evidence of what we teach and how students learn. Evidence creates ownership through student engagement, meaningful learning, and quality teaching.

So the questions become:

- How do we know what music education is?
- How will they know?

Beyond the musician-educators in the system, awareness of our programs should be transparent and understood by students, parents, principals, administrators, community members, school board members, business leaders, and influential organizations (local and afar) who support music, education, creativity and innovation.

This leads to asking two corollary questions:

Question #1:

What do we need to make evident about our music education programs? We need to determine how many students are engaged and involved in our music education programs and if there is a correlation between student achievement data and the students involved in our elective ensembles and courses. Then, we need to publish this information to all stakeholders in our educational community.

Question #2:

How do we do this? By collecting and analyzing data. What kinds of data? And why? We need to collect, interpret, and act upon real-time data which evidence why music is essential and not merely special. The proof is in the data.

In order to effectively manage this process we need to become our own data teams, our own marketing and publications teams in support of music education. To organize, create a vision, and deploy the plan, a group of committed teacher-leaders is essential. One person can not do this alone and shouldn't. Through cultivating teacher-leaders in this process we create ownership, purpose, and value in our music education departments. The value of the whole is realized, and our purpose defined.

So how do we do this? We begin by mining our own data to support our music education programs.

Step 1. Create a data team.
Step 2. Determine what data need to be collected.
Step 3. Make a plan for collection and analysis.
Step 4. Publish the findings.

Data Collection Idea #1

Begin by collecting data on the number of students enrolled in your music education programs. Utilize data collection sheets to determine the percentage of students involved in elective ensembles and courses in the system. Calculate the percentage of students involved. This can be done in many ways: by school, by grade levels, by grade bands, in each genre, by elective course at the secondary level, and for the whole system. A simple excel sheet can be created to do so. Typically creating data sheets by genre is best. Edward S. Lisk, in his book *The Creative Director Conductor, Teacher, Leader,* outlines ways in which to do this, as referenced earlier. The data then need to be collected and managed, essentially creating a larger spreadsheet which houses all of the data collected. As this is done over time, yearly trends can be identified. For example, after three years of data collection the music department can study the overall system-wide data and begin to ask questions like: Has the percentage of students involved in elective music ensembles and courses increased, decreased, or stayed the same? Why? And how do we move forward? What actions need to be taken based upon the data?

Data Collection Idea #2

Compile a list of all concerts and performances in the school system throughout the year. Create a wiki for teachers to list their concerts and performances as a collaborative way to get everyone involved. This is also an efficient way to collect data. Compile and publish this list in an organized creative document and make it a component of your music department annual program assessment report.

Data Collection Idea #3

Utilizing student achievement data, determine the correlations between performance on state assessments and students enrolled in the music education program in your school system. This can be done on many levels. First, each teacher can collect and interpret the data for the students in their schools, and then a larger compilation by grade, school, level, grade band, ensembles and courses can be done.

Marketing What We Do and Why We Do It— the Evidence of Why Music IS Essential in Education:

Marketing what we do and why we do it is essential. As we begin to think about program vision and substantiating why our music education programs are a valuable commodity in our school systems, it is imperative that we educate those who need to be in the know about why music is a meaningful component of student growth and achievement.

Step 1.　Determine the stakeholders who need to be educated about the music education program.

Step 2.　Utilize the three types of data outlined and create an annual assessment of the music education program.

Step 3.　Compile documentation in community-friendly language.

More Food for Thought:

Are annual music education department enrollment goals discussed? Analyzing real-time data supports our music education programs internally as a department. Analysis of data helps us to identify critical issues, needs, and strengths in regard to recruitment and retention. Internal analysis can identify the rigor and relevance of our programs locally and as a whole. When analyzing data internally, critical awareness arises and helps us to determine program needs.

- When does music education move from being a requirement to an elective?
- What impact does this have in regard to retention?
- What impacts do building changes have upon our retention?
- What action do we take based upon the data?

Next Steps:

What can we do beyond data? Marketing, marketing, marketing! Send invitations to every administrator and school board member to every concert. Schedule an appointment with your building administrator to personally invite them to the concert and explain why it is so valuable for them to be at the concert. Share that their support of the students, their families and the school community is important. Sometimes we assume that they just do not want to come. Do we give personal invitations? Have we ever shared a conversation about why it would mean so much to everyone involved in the concert if they were there? Think about being that quality teacher in every facet of what we do and reflect upon who we need to educate about the value of our music education programs.

- If a school system has a local TV channel or radio station, get the word out about upcoming concerts and ask them to record and show the concert. Or ask the radio station if they would do a *Live from Our Concert* broadcast.
- With colleagues, create a CD sampler of systems-wide ensembles throughout the year and gift to your administrators, board members, and community leaders.
- Exposure! Exposure! Exposure! At *all* levels within the school system!
- Get out into the community for concerts! Take your ensembles on the road! Locally! Without transportation expenses! Be creative! And innovative! Collaborate! Find new ways to reach the community through music!

The Recap:

1. Now is the time for systems-wide music department communication and collaboration.
2. Organize your teams: data team, marketing and publications team, concert teams...whatever it takes!

3. Advocate and educate! Use system's evidence to show why music education is a valuable and meaningful, rigorous and relevant component of the system community.

4. Lead the Way! Educate all stakeholders about the value of music in education. Create understanding. This is the opportunity to teach and to move beyond assumption and bias. Make evident WHY music is ESSENTIAL.

Why?

Music is in and within each one of us, inherently innate and creatively expressive; the conscious unconscious which resides as the fabric of our expressive soul.

We are musicians because we connected with music in such a dramatic and passionate way that the choice was almost intrinsically made for us. What we did choose is to teach...and to teach music.

As musician-educators we are a conduit to life. We bring music into the lives of our students so that they may understand the beauty of that which exists in them, within them, and around them every day of their lives.

Give and share your passion every day through music and do so with an insatiable drive and compassion, for we inspire the future.

TIME

Time is like a handful of sand—the tighter you grasp it, the faster it runs through your fingers.

—William Blake

It has been said that there are two kinds of conductors: 'those who handle traffic and those who make music.'

—Frank Battisti, *On Becoming a Conductor*

The direction or energy of thought releases one's artistic considerations.

—Edward S. Lisk, *The Musical Mind of the Creative Director*

Time is one of the most precious commodities for music educators. The countless hours we commit to school are not merely clocked from the first bell to the last each day. We live music. The morning, after school, and weekend rehearsals along with the planning and preparation, logistical and mechanical details which encompass much of what we do makes time a sensitive and all-consuming part of our lives as musician-educators.

When I approach time in both music and life, my philosophy is the following: we must move "through" time in order to move "in" time. For example, I look at my life as a journey through time with me living "in" the moment. I can reflect upon where I have been, and I can look to the future to where I want to go. Right now I am living "in" my life. I own the "in." When I think of the word "over" in relation to life, to me it signifies an end—"it's over"; and/or over is something that is layered on top of something else or remains above. For example, as a goal I live my life to my fullest intents and expectations; and "in" my life, "in" this place of being, breathing, experiencing and expressing, I live "in" each moment of every day to create meaning. "In" is my ownership of my life.

I Approach Music and Teaching in a Similar Way:

As we rehearse a particular piece of music and perform music, we play through the music, literally from point A to point B. And in that music we feel, experience, express, create, and convey meaning. Music to me lives "through" time because it is alive! Whether as one person or an entire ensemble, when we are playing music we are living "in" that experience for a purpose; and this leads to my connection with teaching. There must be meaning and purpose "in" the learning. I have never believed in busy work or just playing a piece of music for the sake of playing it. We must ask ourselves *why* are we doing what we are doing, and thus why we are programming what we are programming, or sightreading, or rehearsing on any given day.

If we want to quantify music "in" time, in my mind I can say that a particular piece of music is played in an anticipated amount of time, perhaps on a continuum. But I never think of playing music over time with students. We play through time because playing music through time is the actual act of collectively collaborating to create music that is beautiful and holds meaning, energized by flow, expressiveness and movement. And yes, in order to move through time, as musicians, I feel we must be able to move in time. When I first began teaching I had a hard time expressing this. As a musician, I had experienced ensembles where we played the music over and over again. "Repeat from measure 1 to 16" and there we went, pounding through the same thing time after time again thinking that the more we played it the better it would get. We were rooted in skills and knowledge. The intended musical learning was void of comprehension, application, and expression. It lacked musical meaning. There is something to be said for using repetition. But this disconnect I am speaking of regarding time is that what we were doing over and over held no value because there was no context or understanding for the musician of why we were doing what we were doing. Sadly, the last thing considered was the beauty of the music and rehearsing as musicians instead of button pushers. The music was missing three vital ingredients: teaching and learning and purpose.

The first time I attended one of Edward S. Lisk's sessions, I experienced one of those moments where everything I had been trying to convey for years to both myself and my students became crystalline and real, and the words and ways in which to approach my teaching became transparent. As he taught us about Internal Pulse and the Ruler of Time, the interconnectedness of each individual in mind/body/spirit was put into words, motion, and music. I perceive that internal pulse accomplishes both moving through and in time and here is why: when we engage students in internal pulse methods, we establish moving in time both individually and collectively. As soon as we are "out" of time, we hear an immediate response that is not moving through time together; and, as we are able to move in time together having established internal pulse, when we transfer this learning to the application of rehearsing and playing a piece of music as an ensemble, we are playing both internally "in" time and externally "through" time to create beautiful music. I feel music as a journey through time and life, not over it.

The ways in which music moves vertically (as we encounter in rhythm and subdivision, and literally in the alignment of voicings/instruments in a score) and horizontally (reading through a piece of music), I apply a scientific/ mathematical approach: if I charted the progression of music happening both horizontally and vertically, music is in constant motion. Music is an interplay of sound and silence. It is always moving forward, or along the continuum, ultimately to me through time, not over time. It is not an end result. In the purest sense music is moving past and beyond, through time, and into the infinite.

Think about a beautiful recital or performing hall for this example. I recall an opportunity I had to perform at the Kimmel Center in Philadelphia. It was the most resonate and warmest hall I had ever performed in. At the conclusion of one of the pieces we played as the final chord sounded, I thought to myself that although the sound to our ears was no longer audible, the energy of the sound remained, floating, soaring, and living through the hall for an amount of time that I could not quantify. I could only perceive it as infinite. Moving away form the analytical, music moving both through and in time in regard to creative/expressive potential must be considered as well. When we speak a sentence, are we speaking through time, over time, or in time? Or in some combination or amalgamation?

When we make an exclamatory statement, to me this happens "in" time, in the "now." When we need to discuss a tough or sensitive situation, or as I sit and try to put my thoughts down on paper here today, I am working through my thoughts. *Through* to me is active. Over is quantifiable, a set amount. Over, to me, is not happening in the now, it is either a perception of what will be or what was.

As little children grow and listen to and experience music, their inner-pulse is developed and motor skills refined allowing for them to mature and learn how to move in time with music. But the premise is that first young children move through time with no specific or fine motor skills. Their movements are large and sweeping, and not necessarily in time. As children mature and their kinesthetic skills develop, the mind/body connection refines their movement and their ability to move in time; seemingly a juxtaposition in our struggle to move older students back to the *through* instead of getting bogged down in the *in*. Through my educational journey, I had the opportunity to teach and participate in infant and preschool music classes. This experience made an impression upon me because I observed infants and preschoolers developmentally refining and maturing motor and kinesthetic, aural, and oral stages of development through music.

I have always been intrigued by the ideas of time, flow, energy, and movement in music; the synergistic interactions of individuals within an ensemble; and their collective creativity, emotion and expressiveness as sculpted and shaped by the conductor. As Edward S. Lisk states in *The Creative Director, Conductor, Teacher, Leader,* "notes remain trivial until they are animated with feeling and spirit." The conductor is the individual who has the responsibility to connect with and allow for communication among the whole, to breathe life through music and to share it with all who are ready to open their hearts and minds and accept the beauty and glory that, I feel, can only be expressed through music.

I attended a concert a couple of years ago where the realization about time once again consumed me as I listened to Grainger's *Horkstow Grange.* The notion of moving "in time" as opposed to moving "through time" caught my attention. From this point to the end of the concert I concentrated on observing how the conductor conducted and the effect/affect that it had on the ensemble. Most of what I observed was conducted "in time"—to the downbeat, to the end of a measure, with little or no movement, flow, or energy happening "through" the phrase, or through the piece in a more global sense. Most of the pieces lived strictly in the "now" of literally each note or each measure. Most were metric and prescribed. I wondered how different the music might have sounded with a change in perspective and/or a change in perhaps conducting and communication with the ensemble.

While the music sounded "together," it could also be described as more of a lock, stop, and barrel approach. There was something to me missing, and again I came back to the words energy, flow, and movement. I wanted the music to go and grow!!! To expand and develop through time!!!

I felt as though the students would have responded amazingly to these subtle changes in perspective. By tweaking one individual's communication with that of the ensemble, the transformation and maturity of the ensemble would have been dramatic. These observations confirmed for me the responsibility that the conductor has to his (or, in my case, her) ensemble.

So for me, music is an interplay and flow of sound and silence energized through time conveying thoughts, feelings, meaning, and purpose to express and deliver a message from one human soul to another.

If you made it this far, THANKS! I appreciate the *time* you have invested.

Purpose

Purpose-filled musical learning is a process, not an event.

—Elizabeth Sokolowski

We make a living by what we get, we make a lifetime by what we give.

—Winston Churchill

Dreams make you click, juice you, turn you on, excite the living daylights out of you. You cannot wait to get out of bed to continue pursuing your dream. The kind of dream I'm talking about gives meaning to your life. It is the ultimate motivator.

—Jim Collins, Good to Great (p. 59)

I shared my personal story earlier about the first ten years of my public education teaching experience. I was a middle school musician-educator, a concert band teacher for 7th, 8th, and 9th grade students. While music is my absolute passion, I felt I could and wanted to do more to support music and the arts in education. I thought to myself, "In the classroom I can annually impact a certain number of students. In a district level position, I can support many teachers who teach hundreds of students, and in doing so, perhaps I can make a greater contribution to education and the role that the arts play in education." The next steps were to complete my masters degree in Educational Leadership and Administration, evolve a role as a learning coordinator for the arts, and then accept a higher-education position to support pre-service musician-educators in their study of teaching through music. Being back to teaching is the best gift I have ever received, professionally. That old adage, "You don't know what your are missing until it is gone" is one that I now appreciate every day. Working with students through the learning process is a must in my life, and being back to it makes my teaching a valuable commodity to me as I serve them in their learning. I have come full circle (at least for now!); I understand my purpose.

Purpose is rooted in student understanding. There must be a fundamental purpose for *what* we choose to do/plan, *how* we deliver the lesson/plan, and *why* it garners purpose for our students. Think carefully as to the choices we make, and the tools which we support as viable and authentic means to benefit students as they grow and mature as musicians. The ways in which they learn and understand *how* to make musical decisions, and the means by which we nurture creative and expressive musicians, individuals, and thinkers are ideals that should be at the forefront of our vision as we chart our future—and that of our students.

Bloom's Taxonomy is a natural compliment of musical learning and musicianship because purpose is in the right place. What I have learned is that in the taxonomy, purpose is the apex of the hierarchy. Even though unstated, it is intended. We are to arrive at purpose as the culmination of the learning, and to transfer ownership of the process from teacher to student. "Here, take this beautiful and meaningful musical experience with you for a lifetime. Remember it, recall it, and use it wisely as you go forth in the world." THIS is the BEAUTY of MUSICAL LEARNING! And yes, I am shouting this out loud, because I am this impassioned about music and how we create purpose for our students. The methodology, pedagogy, and skill sets essential to musical learning and the ability to transfer this notion to all aspects of musicality must be established by setting goals as "summit experiences" (Lisk).

As students learn/mature/develop in regard to methodology and pedagogy, it is our ability to develop and mature specific understandings which transfer to all aspects of musicianship through all pieces of musical literature. This paradigm lifts the ensemble and its members to summit musical experiences as they too own and share in the process of making meaningful, beautiful, and expressive music. As teacher and musician, we fill the role as guide. We must convey to students the purpose (growing to be exceptional musicians), they must be inspired by us (as musician and teacher), and we must cultivate ownership in our students (as collective, expressive, creative, and contributing members of our musical world). We allow for our students to understand musical meaning by building purpose when they are active and engaged learners in our classrooms.

Cultivating Ownership:

> It is an accepted cliche in education that the number one goal of teachers should be to help students learn how to learn. I always see the value in that, sure. But in my mind, a better number one goal was this: I wanted to help students learn how to judge themselves. Did they recognize their true abilities? Did they have a sense of their own flaws? Were they realistic about how others viewed them? In the end, educators best serve students by helping them be more self-reflective. The only way any of us can improve—as Coach Graham taught me—is if we develop a real ability to assess ourselves. If we can't accurately do that, how can we tell if we are getting better or worse?
>
> —Randy Pausch, The Last Lecture,
> pg. 112

Why do students come to school?

- Because of the learning environments which we create...
- Music *is* every person's life, formally and/or informally.
- It surrounds us and is thus all around us, shaping our lives and our core.

- Can you think of a day when you did not hear music? When you did not choose the music you listen to and enjoy?
- Music is a way of life.

For some, music is a filler, an avocation, a prompt, a support, a cultivation, a joyous response to life. For some, music is love. For some, music is passion. For others, music is safety. For many, music is spirit; a celebration of glory, an affirmation of all that is good and just.

And for musicians, music is life. Music defines us, and helps us to sculpt who we are. Music is a voice, a language, a means of communication of all that fills us and fulfills us.

Music is a passion, which for many students is the reason they choose to come to school, as they also choose to be an active musician and maker of creative and personal expression. Music is a means to a greater vision, a hopeful future, a vehicle to break free of confines and to dream big.

Music embraces 21st Century skills, and evidences them through every facet of the engagement of making beautiful music. Music provides students with the opportunity to critically think, to problem solve, to collaborate, to think creatively, and to be innovative.

Our music programs authentically teach music and beyond. We teach skills and values such as time management, self discipline, work ethic, responsibility, peer critique and engagement, social merit, flexibility and adaptability, communication and collaboration, and a differentiated view of life and culture through the music we engage in and interact with.

Music is soul. For many children, the uncovering of their musical "voice" allows for them to understand who they are and gives them the freedom to express, to collaborate, to create, to share, to give—to accept the very soul of whom they are—for music expresses that which can never be said in words.

Music is scientific and mathematical. Music is literacy. Music is historical and resides in the now. Music is reading and writing, it is kinesthetic and inter-/intra-personal, though through a different lens but with the same goals in mind.

Questions for Reflective Contemplation for the Musician-Educator:

Are our musical classrooms environments filled with glorious opportunities? Filled with endless possibilities? In Ben Zander's February 2008 TED Talk, he begins with a wonderful anecdote about two shoe salesmen:

> "Probably a lot of you know the story of the two salesmen who went down to Africa in the 1900s. They were sent down to find if there was any opportunity for selling shoes. And they wrote telegrams back to Manchester. And one of them wrote: 'Situation hopeless. Stop. They don't wear shoes.' And the other one wrote: 'Glorious opportunity. They don't have any shoes yet.'"

The perspective from which we teach directly impacts the learning that students receive. What is your means to cultivate ownership in your classroom? If a student is struggling, do you call it a "situation hopeless" or are you willing to work with that student to help her uncover her musical identity? To help her own her creative musical expression? I have lived in both the "situation hopeless" times and the moments filled with "glorious opportunity". In fact, a "situation hopeless" for me turned into a "glorious opportunity" and helped me to become a better and more thought-filled, purpose-driven teacher.

When I was teaching middle school in the mid-1990s I had a flute student in the 7th grade band who, frankly, I deemed a poor player. What made the situation frustrating was that I am a flute player myself, and no matter what I did, I feel I failed this student while she was a member of my band. She loved band, and participated in as many musical opportunities at school as possible. Something happened, though, over the three years that she was in middle school. Whether she began to practice more or to simply immerse herself in the music program more, her playing started to improve by leaps and bounds. When she entered the 9th grade, she contacted me and asked for me to give her private lessons. She wanted to make district band and also the high school wind ensemble. I had deemed this a "situation hopeless." It was the biggest underestimation of a student I ever made, and a humbling learning experience for me. Assumptions overtook logic, intuition, and heart. We began private lessons and she practiced and practiced and practiced. She became a relentless architect of her own potential. I have never witnessed anything in my time teaching as extraordinary as her drive and determination to fulfill her dreams and goals. She attained her goals and more, even through a serious illness she sustained in high school, and went on to college to study music. This certainly was a lesson learned for me, and a reminder that every student has potential. Do we as musician-educators choose to help all of our students discover their potential? Are we relentless architects? Where do we place our expectations of rigor and relevance in our musical classrooms? For ourselves as musician-educators? For our students as learners? And which population of musical learners are we cultivating?

Much of the focus so far has been on the traditional music education programs established in our systems. On average, this is typically about 20 percent of our student population. But what about the other 80 percent of kids who interact with music every day? How do we bring music education to them in a meaningful and relevant way?

THE OTHER 80 PERCENT

When we first decided to become a musician-educator, it was to teach what we love. Most of us probably envisioned becoming a band director or a vocal music teacher. We got a job and were given our teaching assignments, which might have been paired with another teaching role or responsibility within music, and/or other teaching responsibilities. Perhaps on our journey as a musician-educator we began to teach other courses like music theory, music technology, audio engineering. How many institutions of higher education can you graduate from with a specialized degree to teach K-12 music education in one of these specialized fields? Or how many states have specific certifications for such positions? Our teaching roles evolve as we evolve, as our interests grow and take new forms, as we take on more responsibility or perhaps are given more responsibility or coursework to teach with or without our input.

When I began teaching, I wanted to be a band director and I got a job doing so. In addition to this role, I was assigned to teach 7th and 8th grade general music. As a 22-year-old young woman in her first year of teaching, one of my 8th grade sections of general music was filled with twenty 8th grade boys and myself. I was consumed with covering the curriculum. I was teaching West Side Story and the parallels to Romeo and Juliet and so on and so forth, without much engagement by the boys. What a surprise! What did they want to do? Beat box. They would walk in beat boxing, walk out beat boxing, and every available free minute in class they were beat boxing. As a young teacher this was very frustrating to me. It was *not* in the curriculum! So I spent the entire year squelching their beat boxing; but more importantly and sadly, I neglected their creativity and expression. If only I had thought about how we might incorporate this into what we were learning. How much more meaningful, creative, authentic, and interesting would the experience have become for the boys? How much less frustrated would I have been? Hindsight is always 20/20. It was not that I didn't care, but it was that my true love was in working with the band and this class generally came second in regard to the time I invested planning and preparing. What I realize looking back is that there was an entire other population of creators out there whom I did not reach. Instead I stuck to the confines of the content instead of trying to find ways to cultivate their creativity and self-expression through music and through what they were expected to learn. I was doing a terrible job of reaching the other 80 percent; that is, the rest of the school's population who was not involved in band, chorus, or orchestra. Those who only saw general music as something they had to take because a music course was required.

So how then do we challenge ourselves as creative musician-educators to reach all 100 percent in our school? How do we help all students through music unlock their creative and expressive potential? It is how we blend tradition with innovation. If we want to be 21st Century musician-educators, cultivating all 21st Century learners through music is a priority. When we identify and articulate how we utilize today's learning and innovation skills in our musical classrooms for all learners, we evidence purpose and meaning through music education. We substantiate why music is essential to the school community and in life.

Through music, students learn a wealth about themselves and the ways in which they interact with society, others and life. Students can tap into their expressive and creative capacities to develop their own unique voice if we open our minds and our design to support and nurture this ideal. Musical classrooms create opportunity for students to learn, beyond knowledge and skills, about themselves. Steve Jobs said, "Expose yourself to the best things that humans have to offer and then try to bring those things into what you are doing." Students in our classrooms can uncover what it is they have to offer from within themselves. Their identity, likes, dislikes, strengths, and talents—creatively—are discovered! Where else in education does the personal and unique creative potential that lies within each and every one of our students get discovered? WOW!

Every person is a connoisseur of music. There is not a day when we do not interact with music, whether formally or informally. Music permeates life. We identify our favorite TV shows through music. We remember significant life events through song. Can you imagine a car without a radio? A movie without a soundtrack? Reaching the other 80 percent of our students through music is a critical component to transforming the role of music in education. So how do we do this in a way that reaches their creative and expressive potential? How do we nurture their interests and opinions musically in our classrooms? Through technology.

Ann Curry hosted Voices of Nation this fall on NBC News Education Nation. It was the first time in the history of the program where a panel of students was the focus group interviewed. As a result, a list of 20 Things Students Want the Nation to Know About Education was released. The list can be accessed at http://theinnovativeeducator.blogspot.com. This poignant list evidences the importance of care and community within education that students feel is a critical component of education today, as well as the want and need for teachers to use tools in the classroom which students interact with daily—technological tools, which "makes learning much more interesting." "#16. Bring electives that we are actually interested in back to school. Things like drama, art, cooking, music." Why? Because we are the reasons why students choose to come to school. Our musical environments have the potential and the interest to reach all students, in addition to the traditional 20 percent. Why is this critical information for supporting music in education? When you read the ACOT2 (Apple Classrooms of Tomorrow Today report from 2007) the data on student dropout rates is startling. "1 in 3 high school students do not graduate...1 million students drop out of school every year." There is a clear disconnect between the priorities adults set forward and the needs of our students...our future. Adversity creates opportunity. How will we utilize the message our students are sending us to support them in their future? What does music education for the other 80 percent look like, feel like?

David Sall, an Oberlin College and Conservatory student wrote an article which was published in USA Today called *How to Enliven and Save High School Music.* Here is some major food for thought for musician-educators as he writes, "The primary reason for the dwindling number of students is very likely an ever-increasing disconnect between the traditional band-orchestra-choir conservatory method of teaching—largely geared toward helping students to become professional musicians in classical ensembles—and the way that high school students listen to and experience music today." This is a perfect example of our need to pull the lens back wide and accept that as creative musician-educators we respect the value of the traditional programs we teach *and* we understand the value in being innovative and forward thinking to reach all students through music, to help all students uncover their creative potential.

So the question becomes...How will the integration of technology and music (and beyond!) afford *all* students a lens into their creative, expressive and innovative capacities?

As we acknowledge and use new technology, as we acknowledge and use new and diverse modes of teaching and learning, and as we use our students' real world tools in our classrooms, we bridge the gap between how we were taught and how our students of today need to interface with learning; how we can reach the other 80 percent through enriching and deep musical experiences.

But we must be careful and we must learn about these new forms and how to best reach our 21st Century learners. As Heidi Hayes-Jacobs said in her March 2011 TEDx New York session, "We can do a lot of dumb things with smart boards."

We need to open our eyes wide to the idea of instruction and learning, *driving* the use of technology instead of supplanting it on top of learning to say we are using it. In doing so we empower all students to be creators! We create for 100 percent of the student population valued, meaningful, purpose-filled learning through music as we support our students to uncover their creative and expressive capacities through music.

So what does this look like? Here are some examples:

Music Technology Design:

If you could design the ultimate music app, what would it look like? Sound like? Feel like? What would you be able to do with the app? And why? What does music technology of today look like? What is the course content? What is the goal of the learning in such courses? What types of music technology courses are we offering our students and why?

Music Engagement Courses:

(replaces appreciation)

We redefine research through new forms, moving away from the traditional paper (Hayes-Jacobs) and into a technological approach that interests students. How can our students create podcasts, vodcasts, blogs, and wikis to report out research findings or to give quality feedback about their learning?

- What would Mozart's Facebook page look like?
- What might Sweeny Todd tweet?

Follow 3 composers for 3 weeks on twitter and report your findings. Follow your favorite band on Facebook for a month and report on their musical activity. What are they doing? Where have they been? Why does this interest you?

Hayes-Jacobs calls these *upgrades*, or the replacement of dated content, skills, and assessments. What are the ways in which we can deliver our curriculum and teach the content in a way that reaches our learners through their musical interests and endeavors?

How do we connect our classrooms to the world? Or...how do we bring the world to our classrooms? How do we flatten our sphere of influence? It is all about how resourceful we are. How do we connect with composers and creators via technology? If you ask, they might just video chat!

Hayes-Jacobs says, "We need to be a new kind of teacher." We can do this while respecting tradition and history, as we continue to teach traditional ensembles and in classic teaching environments. But we need to envision the future and how we interact with the rest of our student population, those lovers and engagers of music who do not understand how music can be an interactive and creative environment for them in school. As we begin to reflect upon this vision, we acknowledge moving beyond the doing, the drill, and the practice, and into knowing through creating.

Think back to earlier in this publication when the schematic of Bloom's taxonomy and the idea of purpose was presented. How do we bring purposeful and meaning-filled musical learning to all students in our school community?

Some of the ways in which this is happening today is through service learning projects which support our music programs. If we have a student project team produce a CD of music from diverse schools in the system and sell this to families and community members, we not only make evident all of the music happening in the school but we can collect the proceeds and donate them to an organization in need. Dr. Scott Watson at Parkland High School engages his music technology students annually in a service-oriented project like this. The results are incredible.

There are tremendous opportunities for collaborative and interdisciplinary projects to happen within a school community. When we bring visual artists, musicians, design, writing, technology, and many more school environments together to work on projects, students engage in real-world learning experiences.

One of the coolest scenarios I can envision in a high school is multi-faceted approach to collaborative studies. A course where musicians (who write and perform music) interact with audio engineers (who record the music) and artists and animators create visuals (graphic designers) and communications students film and edit all of the audio and visual material. Students in english classes are writing the scripts and, dependent upon the angle of the project, many other components of the school community can become involved in such projects. Why are courses taught in isolation? Create project management teams and as initiatives are created as truly student-driven opportunities, valued and meaningful learning through the application of their knowledge and skills is taking place.

How do we redefine storytelling? Whether a student musician wants to create a digital portfolio of their repertoire or someone is interested in electronic music who is arranging audio to picture, the possibilities are incredible. How do we enable these students to tell their stories? To show through diverse musical media what music means to them? How do we get students who understand technology—who might not be musicians—engaged in the creative storytelling process? As a portfolio manager, editor, publisher?

The possibilities are limitless. As we allow for our minds to grow wide open, we envision ways to nurture creativity and self expression through music for all students.

Back to Rigor and Relevance for ALL Students through Music:

Now that we have brought into perspective all students and their needs, musically in our educational environments, let's revisit the ideals of a rigorous and relevant music education, but for all students. This understanding begins with a framework developed by Willard Daggett and his staff at the International Center for Leadership in Education. Making connections to the larger contexts of the educational world prove very fruitful in support of our programs. When we establish, through current educational research and models, why music is essential to education, we substantiate our role and purpose through a language administrators and principals can relate to.

The Rigor and Relevance framework is rooted in Bloom's hierarchy of learning (*Knowledge Taxonomy*) and what is called the *Application Model*. When charting the outcomes of synthesizing the concepts of these two continuum, we arrive at the rigor and relevance framework. The framework identifies four quadrants of learning which we authentically assimilate to the music education classroom. The goal is to have students uncovering learning through *Quadrant D*, which engages students in the highest aspects of Bloom's Taxonomy and the Application Model. Quadrant D addresses what Wiggins calls *transfer*, or the ability to take what we have learned and applied, move beyond our current environment, and utilize this learning in new and diverse ways throughout our lives.

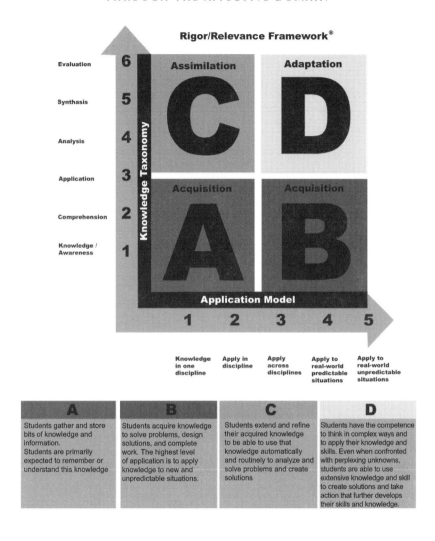

QUADRANT D IS KNOWN AS ADAPTATION

Students have the competence to think in complex ways and to apply their knowledge and skills. Even when confronted with perplexing unknowns, students are able to use extensive knowledge and skill to create solutions and take action that further develops their skills and knowledge.

http://www.leadered.com/rrr.html

CULTIVATING OWNERSHIP

Cultivating ownership allows for us as musician-educators to craft curricula which allows for students to uncover and learn essential skills and knowledge, creating a life-long understanding of music in complex ways. Understandings which may support students as musicians, as appreciators of music, and in diverse facets of their personal and professional lives beyond the musical classroom.

Creating purpose for our musical learners is imperative. A quality music education must be transparent. Student ownership of learning must be a priority and allow for students to learn from mistakes rather then being paralyzed and/or penalized by them.

Have you ever had one of "those" rehearsals? One that from the minute you step in front of the ensemble, things just don't seem right? And from here things only get worse? A rehearsal where time seems to stand still instead of move forward? A rehearsal where, for every one step forward, you feel the ensemble is taking two steps back? Finally you arrive at the end of the rehearsal, and you scratch your head and stare blankly into space wondering what that was with the hopes that it never happens again.

I think it is safe to say we have all experienced the train wreck of a rehearsal in our lifetimes...or at least I hope you have.

Instead of closing the chapter of that book never to read it again, have you ever reflected upon the *whys* of that terrible rehearsal? Was it me? Maybe my planning was terrible? Maybe it was that cold coming on? Was it the students? Were they too busy looking out the windows (if you are lucky enough to have them in your ensemble room) praying for that announcement that we were going home early due to snow? Or was there a disconnect between your expectations as a teacher and the learners in front of you?

Cultivating ownership provides a grand opportunity during such an experience for both teacher and students. When we utilize our miss-takes (Melillo) as valuable and authentic times of disengaged learning and ask both ourselves and our students the *whys* of why this happened, we can move musical learning forward...*together.* Feedback is a powerful learning tool for both teacher and students.

I challenge you, if you have not done so in the past, to return to a not-too-far-distant day of a lousy rehearsal, and engage in a thoughtful discussion with your students about it. Your feedback to students is as critical as their feedback to you. If you are willing to listen and reflect upon student input, you will grow as a teacher. Your students will grow as musicians, and the ownership and responsibility of how that ensemble works collaboratively together to render beautiful music will blossom because students feel as though they too own the music and are not merely decipher-ers of what you as teacher are asking for.

Ensemble is defined by dictionary.com as, "all the parts of anything taken together, so that each part is considered only in relation to the whole." If we expect our students to play in ensemble, then we must cultivate ownership.

In James Jordan's book *The Musician's Soul* he writes:

> Being able to open oneself to the ensemble, to the audience or to the classroom makes an assumption that one can be open to oneself and vulnerable to the world at large. That is, the musician has the ability to be himself devoid of ego, and that he is able to travel to the place within himself where all impulses for making music live. (p. 31)

If the goal of our ensemble is to play in concert, "to plan or act together; acting in a co-ordinated fashion with a common purpose," then we must make evident the meaning of why we are collectively working together, and ownership of this purpose must be transparent and understood by all contributing members.

So how do we cultivate ownership? By inspiring individuals.

Inspiring Individuals

The only man who never makes a mistake is the man who never does anything.

—Theodore Roosevelt

It is Important to develop rehearsal techniques that activate the students' emotional center and encourage feeling to flow through their instruments.

—Edward S. Lisk, *The Creative Director, Conductor, Teacher, Leader*

Before you can inspire with emotion, you must be swamped with it yourself. Before you can move their tears, your own must flow. To convince them, you must yourself believe.

—Winston Churchill

We have many challenges in our midst as we journey on to sustain and grow our musical education programs. But as teachers of this very precious commodity, we also have a responsibility to provide the best for our students with whatever resources we are availed. At the heart of it, music comes from within, and if we believe in our programs and are passionately devoted to this cause called music education, then nothing can stand between us and giving to children of all ages the meaning and value that lies within, around, and among the intangible beauty of music.

For each of us, music at some point in time in our lives became a central and compelling part of our lives, and to such an extent that we trained formally, passed certification exams, and earned degrees which deemed us qualified to bring to our students what was once given to us. It is with this notion that I ask each of us to seriously consider *why* we teach music. As Ken Robinson states, "being good at something isn't a good enough reason to spend your life doing it." (Out of Our Minds, p. 130) How do we pass forward the musical gift which was once given to us? We must teach with passion and compassion, to inspire our students so they will join us in creatively making beautiful music.

In a correspondence I had with a first year high school music teacher, I penned the following…"Love what you do and do what you love. Your energy, compassion, and passion for music is a stepping stone for each and every child who crosses the threshold of the doors to your classroom. And as they step into your musical world, share with them and show them *why* and *how* you developed into such a remarkable and talented musician and person. This is your opportunity, now as teacher, to touch the lives of your students, just as those whom you remember fondly and infinitely touched yours."

To me, we must love being musician-educators. As Stephen Melillo says, we must have a "passionate positive obsession" to bring to students all the ways in which music can impact their lives, and settle for no less. We must show our students, our principals, our community members, and parents how special this gift is, how treasured this musical world has become for the students involved. We must never allow these musical opportunities for our students to be squandered. We must realize we are here to serve our students musically. We must free ourselves of excuses and reasons why we can not succeed and find creative ways to flourish. For in no other area of study can students engage in a creative, emotive, thoughtful, physical, sensitive, complex, mathematical, scientific, and comprehensive educational journey which exists and lives in collectively expressing that which can never be spoken in words; in that which can only be conveyed through music.

In Stephen Melillo's *Let's Find Out Teaching Suite; Hypertools for the Music Educator*, he begins with his philosophy of teaching music which is "You must be better then me." In a wonderfully articulated video clip, Stephen discusses his experiences as a trumpet student. One of the first things his teacher said to him was, "you will never be as good as me." In this film clip, Stephen poignantly examines this statement from a scientific approach, plotting the achievement of his teacher, his achievement, and thus the achievement of all of his subsequent students, and the students of his students on an x-y coordinate graph. What he arrives at by charting the perspective of his trumpet teacher is that music, and the learning and teaching of it, will end in total self-destruction if the trumpet teacher's philosophy is utilized (I believe Steve actually uses the words *dark, dismal, death*). He turns this statement around and tells his students, "you *must* be better than me." By doing so, we have created infinite human potential through music.

Stephen states, "In my life as a student, nothing has so motivated me as an efficient learning process that respects time while allowing me to achieve measurably and with substance." I encourage you to check out Stephen Melillo s teaching tools and music at www.stormworld.com.

How do you inspire your students? How do you make meaning? How do you journey to the summit of creative musical expression with your students? Edward S. Lisk states:

> It is the 'I' that holds the answer...
>
> It is the 'I' that cannot be copied, imitated, or contrived...
>
> The 'I' found in the Intangible, Intrinsic, Inherent and the Innate...
>
> The 'I' words are connected through musical 'I'magination...
>
> A musical imagination that speaks through the beauty of sound...
>
> Moving in and out of silence!
>
> (February 1996)

Edward S. Lisk and Stephen Melillo are two beacons of light in my journey as a musician-educator. To me, the beauty that these two men bring to the world through music and the ways in which they share and give music to others is a crystalline embodiment of teacher. Their mentorship and collegiality has helped me to grow, and the most beautiful result of this is what I am able to give and share with my students. I encourage you to invest your time in their teaching tools for the benefit of your student musicians.

How do we nurture creativity in our student musicians? Through our decisions which creatively address the choices we make, the how and why and when we engage students musically, through what we are doing and not doing, in what we are supporting and not supporting; from the cultivation of emotion, creativity, and musical expression, and when we afford our students the musical opportunities to be beautiful and giving individuals through music.

Music is complex and beautiful. Music conveys that which can never be spoken in words. Our role as teacher is to provide students with the diverse and interconnected gift of all that music can bring into their lives.

- What will you choose to do?
- What type of teacher will you choose to be?
- What type of classroom environment will you create?
- How will you allow for your students to tap into their creative potential and find their musical voice?

Here is a "thank you" that Edward S. Lisk shared with me which epitomizes why we do what we do, when we give of ourselves to music and our students:

> Your affect on the wind band conducting world over the past two decades has been and continues to be profound. Watching you teach and conduct during this residency was a reminder of how important it is to have command of what we do, but most importantly, to have a deep love of

music and of musicians. When those aspects of teaching are combined, then and only then, magic is the result.

I know that the students were enamored with you, your love of music, your wonderful work, and your considerate and passionate comments to them. They are, as you so beautifully stated, the future of our profession. When they learn to love music in a sincere manner, and when they find the magic that lies within themselves, their dreams will begin to be realized.

Beautiful people make beautiful music; beautiful music makes beautiful people.

Remember Winston Churchill's statement? "We make a living by what we get, we make a life by what we give."

So what are the means by which we can give to our students? First and foremost, through our dedication and thoughtful planning and preparation for our musical classrooms. Second, through the ways in which we support and nurture the creativity and self-expression of our student musicians.

NURTURING CREATIVITY
AND SELF-EXPRESSION

Finding and developing our creative strengths is an essential part
of becoming who we really are. We don't know who we can be
until we know what we can do.

—Ken Robinson, *The Element (p. 23)*

Insight is not a lightbulb that goes off inside our heads. It is a
flickering candle that can easily be snuffed out.
—Malcolm Gladwell, *Blink*

Our musical environments avail us of endless opportunities to tap into
the intangible potential of every student in our schools. Music summons all
students to be creative, imaginative and innovative. The challenge is *how*
we choose to allow for students to be inspired and expressive, and how we
nurture and support their growth through music as individuals.

To engage students in the transformative process of creativity we
must not squander their opportunities to think imaginatively, for this
is the beginning of the creative process. The means by which we deliver a
musical curricula and the connections we provide as musician-educators for
engagement in higher levels of Bloom's Taxonomy develop creative capacities.

Musical classroom environments allow for students to be responsible for their learning and incorporate both the effectual (thinking - decision making) and the affectual (feeling - emoting). This journey of making musical meaning which celebrates creativity, engagement, and innovation is a joint venture between and among students and teachers.

The easy route is to enable, to feed students the rote information they need to be successful at the doing. But this success will, in the end, be squandered as there is no substance behind it. It lacks knowing and understanding. Musical learning must allow *for* students to think and process, to search and question, to build the determination and inner drive fostered by experience and environment as essential means through which development and maturation is an outcome, not a chance. The convergence of cognition and expression cultivates life-long values and understandings in our students. Music transcends all disciplines and is interdisciplinary in nature. Music is mathematical and scientific; it is historical. Music develops comprehension, reading, aural, oral, and conceptual skills. Music is kinesthetic, linguistic, interpersonal and intrapersonal. It promotes imaginative inquiry, improvisation, creative thinking and feeling, and leads to the development of highly innovative individuals.

Every human being is a consumer of music in some capacity, the variable is the extent to which individuals are aware of this. Our challenge is to influence the perception of those students we tag superficially as "non-performers," allowing for them to realize the spectrum of ways in which music exists in their lives, thus unlocking their imaginative and creative potential.

Our musical classrooms are the places where students find their identity, where they often discover their meaning and purpose. Our classrooms provide students the learning styles and schemes that allow for understanding and knowledge to compliment creative expression through application. Musical classrooms are the reasons *why* our students become involved and contributing members of their school communities and *how* they prepare themselves for the future. Our classrooms are the places where many students literally "find their voices." "Our creative capacities are released and realized through the medium we use. Discovering the right medium is often a tidal moment in the creative life of an individual" (*Out of Our Minds*, p. 129). If we do not provide the opportunities necessary for students to find their path and to support it, then the educational process has neglected its primary intents. We have a primary responsibility to find creative solutions to obstacles and to move beyond excuses and into action.

21ST CENTURY LEARNING AND THE IMPACT OF TECHNOLOGY INTEGRATION IN MUSIC

Young Americans coming of age in this century—the 70 million people born between 1982 and 2000—live in a world that is dramatically more complex than it was just a few years ago. In a remarkably short period of time, the world and its people, economies, and cultures have become inextricably connected, driven largely by the Internet, innovations in mobile computers and devices, and low-cost telecommunications technology. This global interdependence has profound implications for all aspects of American society—from how we think and work to how we play and learn.

—Apple Classrooms of Tomorrow...Today
(ACOT 2) April 2008

Our 21st Century learners are digital natives. They are equipped and technologically knowledgeable and creative consumers. As digital immigrants, we live and educate in times very different from when we were students (think about the evolution of the telephone over your lifetime, as one example of how quickly technology is transforming the ways in which we live and interact with others). The world has made this transformation to what is coined as the creative age, the creative economy, the age of innovation, and we must approach learning and interaction with our students to best serve their needs in this time. We must take measures to understand their world and engage with them in learning opportunities which connect with their ubiquitous technological realities.

This age of creativity releases our students from the confines of education built upon an industrial model and into a world where anything and everything is possible. The perception among our students today is that anything and everything now is possible—seemingly instantaneously! As my 11 year old daughter says to me everyday, "But Mom, nothing is impossible!" The rate at which technology is evolving and the unpredictability of what is to come leaves us in a world which is unfamiliar and unchartered for all. As Ken Robinson says in his 2006 TED talk, we are educating children now for jobs that do not even exist yet! Think about how profound that statement is! For the first time in history, technology is outpacing us. We are educating millions of students every year, preparing them for their future; and much of what they might be doing is not in existence today.

- How does this impact our classrooms?
- How does this impact the ways in which students learn?
- How does this impact our musical classrooms where methodological study and practice is required?

If we reframe these questions and embrace the potential of our students and recognize how and why and what we teach needs to be designed in a way to reach these 21st Century learners, then we must also acknowledge and learn about their technology. Authentic utilization of technology can serve to support a musical education without acting as an imposition or replacement for it.

In Ken Robinson's book *The Element* he redefines creativity and intelligence in a way to support our 21st Century learners. He moves away from the stigmatism of intelligence simply being a number and creativity being something that is answered as a yes or no question. Albert Einstein says, "imagination is more important than knowledge." The beauty for a mathematician is not in arriving at the final correct answer. The beauty lies in the creative process utilized to arrive at an end result. It's all about the process! So if we ask about intelligence in terms of understanding, the question then becomes *how are you intelligent?* If we reflect upon this question in regard to music, we open up an incredible world of musical possibility to all students, not just those deemed "gifted" or "talented." Every child is intelligent in some way. Our goal as teachers is to help them to unlock their intellectual potential. Learning for intelligence is a point of departure in which we nurture students through discovery to creatively understand how their learning brings meaning to their lives and helps them to grow intellectually.

Robinson defines intelligence in three ways. It is diverse; we have unlimited intelligent potential, and so do our students. Intelligence is dynamic; our intelligence is intensely interactive, and so is that of our students. Intelligence is distinctive; it is "as unique as a fingerprint," and so is that of our students. (Robinson, *The Element*).

The connection between creativity and intelligence is like a superhighway, converging as these two once separable factors are now seen as inseparable and vital to one another. Creativity is so often stereotyped by adults and children as those "creators" who excel at something artistic. Our definition of creativity has been limited, and this inhibits the potential of every student we interact with. If we change the lens and think of creativity beyond a "yes you have it or no you don't" type of mentality, we open up to the idea that all students are creative. Our job as teacher is to cultivate every child's potential and unlock their unique self. So the question becomes, for ourselves and our students, how are we creative?

Creativity is the ability to transcend traditional ideas, rules, and patterns. It is originality. Creativity is active! It involves the energy of doing, of being creative in something! Creativity involves action and is the application of imagination! Creativity is "actively producing something in a deliberate way." (Robinson, p. 115) Creativity is a process, not an isolated event. The ways in which we cultivate our students' intelligence, cognition, and intellect is through opening up endless possibilities through their imagination, which sparks a creative process, resulting in an innovative experience and/or product.

Creativity begins with imagination, as we form mental images or concepts of what is not physically present to the senses. That which is "in the mind's eye." Creativity leads to innovation when we make imagination and creativity a reality. Innovation is being passionate about something by putting creativity into practice.

Think about when NASA first put a man on the moon. The basis of this example comes from a session Stephen Melillo did with a room filled with musician-educators. He calls this *The NASA Principle*. The goal is stated *first*, and the then the backward design to the goal is derived by logic. As he passionately exclaimed to the group, "NASA did not just think about it! They did it!" NASA determined their target, charted a path, and made it happen. When you begin with an idea in your imagination. Do you think we can put a man on the moon? This leads to the process of developing that imaginative idea creatively. Let's come up with a plan and the necessary apparatus to put a man on the moon. This creative action is then defined by the development of the imaginative idea through the creative process in the evolution of a new innovation, in this case Apollo 11.

So how do we apply these ideals to learning? And more specifically musical learning? It is through how we teach. In Grant Wiggins' model, it is the acquisition of knowledge and skills, making meaning for purpose, and the transfer of understanding to new and more sophisticated context. This directly relates back to our discussion of Bloom's Taxonomy, and the ideal that we teach for purpose. What do you want your students to learn beyond skills and knowledge so that they can actually apply this learning to diverse situations? And how does this relate to what we do on a daily basis as musician-educators? Teaching through the 21st Century skills framework, supported by Bloom's Taxonomy and the Understanding by Design model, provides us with an opportunity to make meaning of the discrete facts and skills being taught in isolation.

The "arts" are a key component of the core subjects and 21st Century themes developed by the *Partnership for 21st Century Learning* in their skills framework. There are two components of skills which music strongly correlates with. To support our music education programs, making evident the ways in which these skills components link to the national standards for music education as well as how these are an authentic outgrowth of music and how students learn in a musical environment, we further substantiate the necessity of music in our schools.

The first skill set deals with learning and innovation skills. It is identified as *creativity and innovation, critical thinking and problem solving*, and *communication and collaboration*. The graphs below link these skills to the national standards for music education and musical learning.

Creativity and Innovation	A musical means to these skills...
Think creatively	Performing solo or in ensemble
Work creatively with others	Engaging in ensemble
Implement innovations	Improvising, composing, arranging

Critical Thinking and Problem Solving	A musical means to these skills...
Communicate clearly	Reading notation and producing music
Use systems thinking	Reading and analyzing music
Make judgments and decisions	Making musical and expressive decisions
Solve problems	Studying and rehearsing music

Communication and Collaboration	A musical means to these skills...
Communicate clearly with others	Expressing yourself musically
Collaborate with others	Playing/singing in ensemble
Collaborate with others	Understanding the relationship between music and other arts, history and culture

Life and Career Skills	A musical means to these skills...
Flexibility and adaptability	Engaging in ensemble
Initiative and self-direction	The discipline of studying/practicing music and primary instrument
Social and cross-cultural skills	Understanding the relationship between music and other arts, history and culture
Productivity and accountability	Musical performance solo and in ensemble
Leadership and responsibility	The art of being a musician

When music is an essential element in the educational lives of our students, we prepare them yes, as musicians, but we give them the skills and tools to be expressive and unique individuals epitomizing the essence of the 21st Century skills framework. In Tom Peters' book *The Circle of Innovation*, creative and innovative businesses which have transformed the ways in which we think about the systems approach are identified. He states that "we are all Michelangelos." In other words, everyone has unique creative potential. We have moved out of industrialism and training for a specific skill. Truly innovative businesses of the 21st Century are not hiring individuals for a skill. They are hiring for their abilities to be creative and innovative critical thinkers and problem solvers. Businesses will spend millions of dollars training their employees in their specific skill set or means of production, but they are hiring for those who can look beyond and be innovators. We must expose students to these learning and innovation skills, and cultivate their abilities to be independent, efficient, and exceptional thinkers. Music is a means to this evolution!

Peters states, "Hire for diversity, train for whatever. Hire for attitude, train for whatever. Hire for attitude, train for skill. Hire for intelligence (all kinds), train for whatever. Be a connoisseur of talent." These are the individuals he calls the WOW-ERS! Music is distinctive, dynamic, and diverse, and through music students learn not only the discrete skills needed to produce music, they learn and understand how to expressively create music. A truly dynamic musician-educator is able to bring these understandings to students fundamentally so that students can make meaning of their learning and transfer their acquisition of musical knowledge to all facets of their lives. When we can identify and articulate how we integrate these learning and innovation skills into our musical classrooms and when we evidence purpose and meaning through music education to support 21st Century learners, we substantiate why music is essential to the school environment and community...and in life.

CHOICE

As musician-educators, we embrace the 21st Century skills and utilize creativity and intelligence to help students discover their element. We bring meaning and direction to the lives of our students. Ken Robinson coins the word element to "describe that place where the things we love to do and the things we are good at come together." To me, this *is* music. Remember that saying that hangs in my office which I see every day when I open my door? Do what you love and love what you do. Fulfill your purpose in life and inspire your students to discover their potential.

Why do we teach? To leave footprints upon our students' minds and hearts as hopeful steps into the future, inspiring creative paths of their own. Make your life through what you give. How will you choose to live? How do you choose to bring music into the life of every student who walks through your classroom door? How will you help your students unlock their creative and expressive potential so that they are inspired to live life fully? As musician-educators we are a conduit to life. We bring music into the lives of our students so that they may understand the beauty of that which exists in them, within them, and around them every day of their lives. Be an architect of human potential; give and share your passion every day through the beauty of music and do so with an insatiable drive and compassion, for we are inspiring the future.

How do our decisions creatively address the choices we make? How and why and when do we engage students? What we are doing and not doing? What are we teaching and not teaching? What we are supporting and not supporting? How does music impact and inspire emotion, creativity, and expression? And *why* is this essential to education?

Love what you do and do what you love. Your energy, compassion, and passion for music is a stepping stone for each and every student who crosses the threshold of the doors of your classroom. And as they step into your world, share with them and show them why and how you developed into such a remarkable musician and teacher.

The choice...is yours.

WORKS CITED

Apple. *Apple Classrooms of Tomorrow...Today: Leaning in the 21ˢᵗ Century.* Apple, 2008, p. 6.

Battisti, Frank. *On Becoming a Conductor.* Maryland: Meredith Music Publications, 2007, pp. vii, 51, 82.

Bransford, John D., Ann L. Brown, and Rodney C. Cocking. *How People Learn: Brain, Mind, Experience, and School.* Washington, DC: The National Academic Press, 2000, p. 224.

Coffey, Heather. Website: www.learnnc.orf/lp/pages/4719

Collins, Jim. *Good to Great: Why Some Companies Make the Leap...and Others Don't.* New York: HarperCollins Publishers, Inc., 2001, pp. 59, 128.

Danielson, Charlotte. *Enhancing Professional Practice: A Framework for Teaching.* Second edition. Virginia: ASCD, 2007, p. 1.

DuFour, Richard, and Robert Eaker. *Professional Learning Communities at Work: Best Practices for Enhancing Student Achievement.* Virginia: ASCD, 1998.

Gladwell, Malcolm. *Blink.* New York: Little, Brown, and Company, 2005, p. 122.

Hayes-Jacobs, Heidi. *Curriculum 21: Essential Education for a Changing World.* Virginia: ASCD, 2010.

International Center for Leadership. *Rigor and Relevance Framework.* Website: www.leadered.com/rrr.html

Jordan, James, *The Musician's Soul.* Chicago: GIA Publications, Inc., 1999, p. 31.

Levitin, Daniel J. *This Is Your Brain on Music: The Science of Human Obsession.* New York: PLUME, 2006, p. 9.

Lisk, Edward S. *The Creative Director: Conductor, Teacher, Leader.* Maryland: Meredith Music Publications, 2006, pp. 10, 60, 88.

------. *The Musical Mind of the Creative Director.* Maryland: Meredith Music Publications, 2010, pp. 8, 13, 38.

Marzano, Robert, Debra Pickering, and Jane Pollack. *Classroom Instruction that Works.* First edition. Virginia: ASCD, 2001, p. 30.

Melillo, Stephen. *Let's Find Out Teaching Suite: Hypertools for the Music Educator.* Virginia: STORMWORKS. Website: www.stormworld.com

New Jersey Standards Clarification Project. Website: http://www.state.nj.us/education/aps/njscp/

Partnership for 21st Century Skills. Website: www.p21.org

Pausch, Randy. *The Last Lecture.* New York: Hyperion, 2008, pp. 79, 112, 138.

Pennsylvania Standards Aligned System. Website: www.pde.sas.org

Peters, Tom. *The Circle of Innovation.* New York: Vintage Books, 1997, pp. 123, 144, 145, 368, 370, 372, 374, 377.

------. *TP's "Top 41 Quotes."* No. 41. Website: www.tompeters.com

Pink, Daniel. *A Whole New World: Moving from the Information Age to the Conceptual Age.* New York: Riverhead Books, 2005, pp. 21, 35.

------. *Drive: The Surprising Truth about What Motivates Us.* New York: Riverhead Books, 2009, p. 56.

Robinson, Ken. *Out of Our Minds: Learning to Be Creative.* United Kingdom: Capstone Publishing Limited, 2001, p. 130.

------. *The Element: How Finding Your Passion Changes Everything.* New York: Viking, 2009, pp. 23, 115.

------. Website: www.ted.com (accessed February 2010).

Smith, Jeffrey K., Lisa F. Smith, and Richard DeLisi. *Natural Classroom Assessment: Designing Seamless Instruction and Assessment*. California: Corwin Press, Inc., 2001, pp. 48, 51.

Taylor, Bruce D. *The Skills Connection Between the Arts and 21st Century Learning*. Education Week. Online edition accessed February 1, 2011.

Wiggins, Grant, and Jay McTighe. *Understanding by Design*. Second edition. Virginia: ASCD, 2005, pp. 7, 14, 41, 46, 49, 69.

Zander, Benjamin. Website: www.ted.com (accessed February 2008).

Zander, Rosamund, and Benjamin Zander. *The Art of Possibility*. New York: Penguin Books, 2000.

—ABOUT THE AUTHOR—

Elizabeth Sokolowski is Head of the Music Education Division of the School of Music at the University of the Arts in Philadelphia, PA. Mrs. Sokolowski is responsible for the curricular components of the Music Education Program and teaches graduate level courses in K-12 Music, Curriculum Design, Assessment, Music Pedagogy and Methodology, and Music Technology. A graduate of Temple University with a Bachelor of Music in Music Education degree, she has attended graduate studies at the University of the Arts, West Chester and Villanova Universities, and earned a Masters degree at St. Joseph's University from the Educational Leadership and Educational Administrative and Supervisory Program. Mrs. Sokolowski holds a Pennsylvania Instructional II Teaching Certificate and a Pennsylvania Administrative and Supervisory Certificate. In addition to her role at the University of the Arts, Mrs. Sokolowski presents at state and national music conferences on Current Trends in Music Education, Music Technology Integration, Curriculum Design and Development, Assessment, Instruction and 21st Century Learning and Creativity in Music Education. Mrs. Sokolowski has presented at the Midwest Band and Orchestra Clinic, the Pennsylvania Music Educators Annual Conference and Summer Conference, District 12 PMEA Election Day Inservice Days, varied school district inservices, at the Technology Institute for Music Educators State and National Conferences, and at the Conn-Selmer Institute.

Mrs. Sokolowski holds membership in the Pennsylvania Music Educators Association (PMEA), the Music Educators National Conference (MENC), the Technology Institute for Music Educators (TI:ME), and the Association for Supervision and Curriculum Development (ASCD).

Elizabeth Sokolowski
The University of the Arts
School of Music
Division Head of Music Education
320 South Broad Street
Philadelphia, PA 19102
esokolowski@uarts.edu

—Advance Reviews—

Edward S. Lisk,
Conductor, Clinician, Author
Oswego, NY

Elizabeth Sokolowski's newest publication, MAKING MUSICAL MEANING, is a significant contribution to our music profession as education continues its transformation. Elizabeth presents a new paradigm for designing a comprehensive music education program that is extremely important for music program survival. Her vision is based on her philosophy of music that has evolved through her career as a public school music teacher, administrator, and extensive research. Elizabeth provides a solid foundation for young and old educators in bringing the joy and beauty of music to all students. This publication is simply a powerful book that is required reading for all music educators.

Johanna J. Siebert, Ph.D.
Chair, National Council of Supervisors of Music Education
Director of Fine Arts, Webster Central School District, NY

In *Making Musical Meaning*, Elizabeth Sokolowski shares her passion for principled, informed music teaching and learning. Here, readers are inspired and empowered to implement instruction that yields true understanding and self-satisfaction for today's music students. She is insightful in her relation of high quality musical experiences to a solid grounding in 21st Century Skills, and makes the case well for the benefits of prolonged participation in music-making to creativity, innovation, collaboration, and communication. Beth Sokolowski's convincing arguments have contributed to my lack of confidence in school districts' short-sighted budget-making decisions that continue to marginalize the arts; moreover, she's caused me to wonder how non-musicians will even begin to prepare for the uncertainties of a rapidly changing world and job market! This book should be on the mandatory reading list for any college music education major, and for those in positions of music leadership, anywhere.

R. David Orehowsky
Director of Bands, Pennfield Middle School
North Penn School District, PA

Beth Sokolowski is a dedicated and passionate music educator whose insight and vision have led her to "keep one foot in the present and an eye on the future." *Making Musical Meaning...* provides strategies for creating the necessary structure to look toward the future in support of the rigor, relevance, sustainment, and growth of a comprehensive music curriculum. Beth's book reminds music educators to continually examine both why and what they do, poses questions for reflective contemplation, and encourages us all to become architects of our own potential, while inspiring our students to do the same.

Dr. Richard Mayne
Professor of Music/Associate Director of Bands
University of Northern Colorado

Elizabeth Sokolowski's, "Making Musical Meaning" illustrates her vast knowledge of music and sheer intellect. In addition, her passion for insisting that Music is a fundamental component to the educational curriculum is paramount. This new book is thought provoking, and a sign that certainly there is more to come from this author.

Stephen Melillo
Composer

In the end, as well as in the beginning, nothing beats Sincerity. Sincerity in Purpose. Sincerity in Focus. Sincerity in Work. With Sincerity in Heart, all that follows is the best that you can give. Elizabeth Sokolowski's book is a combined outpouring of autobiography, history, reflective research, forward-thinking and hope-filled inspiration for the future of Music Education. In her, *Making Musical Meaning*, Elizabeth provides a pedagogical and impassioned mirror in which we can take stock of ourselves, Re-examine our philosophies and re-evaluate our objectives.

Marc Dicciani
Director of the School of Music, The University of the Arts
Philadelphia, PA

Elizabeth Sokolowski is a combination of all the things required to be a great teacher—a compassionate, passionate, creative, enthusiastic, critical thinker, who cares about her subject, and cares more about her students. In her book, *Making Musical Meaning*, Beth weaves personal stories, teaching and administrative experience, and extensive research together with the principles of meaning, value, purpose, change, and vision. In so doing, she builds a blueprint for a successful and fulfilling life as a teacher, and an exciting journey towards your own deeper meaning.